Jane Austen's sailor brothers: being the adventures of Sir Francis Austen ... and ... Charles Austen;

John Henry Hubback, Edith Charlotte Hubback

BIBLIOLIFE

JANE AUSTEN'S
SAILOR BROTHERS

Being the Adventures of Sir Francis
Austen, G.C.B., Admiral of the Fleet
and Rear-Admiral Charles
Austen By J. H. Hubback
and Edith C. Hubback

mdccccvi
London: John Lane
The Bodley Head, Vigo Street, W.
New York: John Lane Company

TO M. P. H.

"I HAVE DISCOVERED A THING VERY
LITTLE KNOWN, WHICH IS THAT IN
ONE'S WHOLE LIFE ONE CAN NEVER
HAVE MORE THAN ONE MOTHER.
YOU MAY THINK THIS OBVIOUS.
YOU ARE A GREEN GOSLING!"

PREFACE

PERHAPS some apology may be expected on behalf
of a book about Jane Austen, having regard to
the number which have already been put before
the public in past years. My own membership of
the family is my excuse for printing a book which
contains little original matter, and which might be
described as "a thing of shreds and patches," if
that phrase were not already over-worked. To
me it seems improbable that others will take a
wholly adverse view of what is so much inwoven
with all the traditions of my life. When I recollect my childhood, spent chiefly in the house of
my grandfather, Sir Francis, and all the interests
which accompanied those early days, I find myself
once more amongst those deep and tender dis-
tances. Surrounded by reminiscences of the
opening years of the century, the Admiral always
cherished the most affectionate remembrance of
the sister who had so soon passed away, leaving

Jane Austen's Sailor Brothers

those six precious volumes to be a store of household words among the family.

How often I call to mind some question or answer, expressed quite naturally in terms of the novels; sometimes even a conversation would be carried on entirely appropriate to the matter under discussion, but the actual phrases were "Aunt Jane's." So well, too, do I recollect the sad news of the death of Admiral Charles Austen, after the capture, under his command, of Martaban and Rangoon, and while he was leading his squadron to further successes, fifty-six years having elapsed since his first sea-fight.

My daughter and I have made free use of the *Letters of Jane Austen*, published in 1884, by the late Lord Brabourne, and wish to acknowledge with gratitude the kind permission to quote these letters, given to us by their present possessor. In a letter of 1813, she speaks of two nephews who "amuse themselves very comfortably in the evening by netting; they are each about a rabbit-net, and sit as deedily to it, side by side, as any two Uncle Franks could do." In his octogenarian days Sir Francis was still much interested in this same occupation of netting, to protect his Morello

Preface

cherries or currants. It was, in fact, only laid aside long after his grandsons had been taught to carry it on.

My most hearty thanks are also due to my cousins, who have helped to provide materials for our work; to Miss M. L. Austen for the loan of miniatures and silhouettes; to Miss Jane Austen for various letters and for illustrations; to Commander E. L. Austen for access to logs, and to official and other letters in large numbers; also to Miss Mary Austen for the picture of the *Peterel* in action, and to Mrs. Herbert Austen, and Captain and Mrs. Willan for excellent portraits of the Admirals, and to all these, and other members of the family, for much encouragement in our enterprise.

JOHN H. HUBBACK.

July 1905.

CONTENTS

LIST OF ILLUSTRATIONS

List of Illustrations

JANE AUSTEN'S
SAILOR BROTHERS

CHAPTER I

BROTHERS AND SISTERS

No one can read Jane Austen's novels, her life, or her letters; without feeling that to her the ties of family were stronger and more engrossing than any others.

Among the numbers of men and women who cheerfully sacrifice the claims of their family in order that they may be free to confer somewhat doubtful benefits on society, it is refreshing to find one who is the object of much love and gratitude from countless unknown readers, and who yet would have been the first to laugh at the notion that her writing was of more importance than her thought for her brothers and sister, or the various home duties which fell to her share. It is this sweetness and wholesomeness of thought, this clear conviction that her "mission" was to do her duty, that gives her books and letters their peculiar quality. Her theory of life is clear. Whatever troubles befall, people must go on doing their work and making the best of it; and we are not allowed to feel respect, or even overmuch sympathy, for the characters in the novels who cannot bear this test. There is a matter-of-courseness about this view which, combined with all that we know of the other members of the family, gives one the idea that the children at Steventon had a strict bringing up. This, in fact, was the case, and a very rich reward was the result. In a family of seven all turned out well, two rose to the top of their profession, and one was—Jane Austen.

The fact of her intense devotion to her family could not but influence her writing. She loved them all so well that she could not help thinking of them even in the midst of her work ; and the more we know of her surroundings, and the lives of those she loved, the more we understand of the small joyous touches in her books. She was far too good an artist, as well as too reticent in nature, to take whole characters from life ; but small characteristics and failings, dwelt on with humorous partiality, can often be traced back to the natures of those she loved. Mary Crawford's brilliant letters to Fanny Price remind one of Cassandra, who was the "finest comic writer of the present age." Charles' impetuous disposition is exaggerated in Bingley, who says, "Whatever I do is done in a hurry," a remark which is severely reproved by Darcy (and not improbably by Francis Austen), as an "indirect boast." Francis himself comes in

Brothers and Sisters

for his share of teasing on the opposite point of his extreme neatness, precision, and accuracy. " They are so neat and careful in all their ways," says Mrs. Clay, in " Persuasion," of the naval profession in general ; and nothing could be more characteristic of Francis Austen and some of his descendants than the overpowering accuracy with which Edmund Bertram corrects Mary Crawford's hasty estimate of the distance in the wood.

" ' I am really not tired, which I almost wonder at ; for we must have walked at least a mile in this wood. Do not you think we have ? '

" ' Not half a mile,' was his sturdy answer ; for he was not yet so much in love as to measure distance, or reckon time, with feminine lawlessness.

" ' Oh, you do not consider how much we have wound about. We have taken such a very serpentine course, and the wood itself must be half a mile long in a straight line, for we have never seen the end of it yet since we left the first great path.'

" ' But if you remember, before we left that first great path we saw directly to the end of it. We looked down the whole vista, and saw it closed by iron gates, and it could not have been more than a furlong in length.'

" ' Oh, I know nothing of your furlongs, but I am sure it is a very long wood ; and that we have been winding in and out ever since we came into it ; and therefore when I say that

3

we have walked a mile in it I must speak within compass.'

" 'We have been exactly a quarter of an hour here,' said Edmund, taking out his watch. 'Do you think we are walking four miles an hour?'

" 'Oh, do not attack me with your watch. A watch is always too fast or too slow. I cannot be dictated to by a watch.'

" A few steps farther brought them out at the bottom of the very walk they had been talking of.

" ' Now, Miss Crawford, if you will look up the walk, you will convince yourself that it cannot be half a mile long, or half half a mile.'

" ' It is an immense distance,' said she; ' I see that with a glance.'

" ' He still reasoned with her, but in vain. She would not calculate, she would not compare. She would only smile and assert. The greatest degree of rational consistency could not have been more engaging, and they talked with mutual satisfaction.' "

It is in "Mansfield Park" and in "Persuasion" that the influence of her two sailor brothers, Francis and Charles, on Jane Austen's work can be most easily traced. Unlike the majority of writers of all time, from Shakespeare with his "Seacoast of Bohemia" down to the author of a penny dreadful, Jane Austen never touched, even lightly, on a subject unless she had a real knowledge of its

Brothers and Sisters

details. Her pictures of the life of a country
gentleman and of clergymen are accurate, if not
always sympathetic. Perhaps it was all too near
her own experience to have the charm of romance,
but concerning sailors she is romantic. Their very
faults are lovable in her eyes, and their lives
packed with interest. When Admiral Croft, Captain Wentworth, or William Price appears on the
scene, the other characters immediately take on a
merely subsidiary interest, and this prominence is
always that given by appreciation. The distinction awarded to Mr. Collins or Mrs. Elton, as the
chief object of ridicule, is of a different nature.
The only instance she cared to give us of a sailor
who is not to be admired is Mary Crawford's
uncle, the Admiral, and even he is allowed to earn
our esteem by disinterested kindness to William
Price.

No doubt some of this enthusiasm was due to
the spirit of the times, when, as Edward Ferrars
says, "The navy had fashion on its side"; but
that sisterly partiality was a stronger element there
can be no question. Her place in the family was
between these two brothers, Francis just a year
older, and Charles some four years younger. Much
has been said about her fondness for "pairs of
sisters" in her novels, but no less striking are the
"brother and sister" friendships which are an
important factor in four out of her six books. The

5

Jane Austen's Sailor Brothers

love of Darcy for his sister Georgina perhaps suggests the intimacy between James Austen and Jane, where the difference in their ages of ten years, their common love of books, the advice and encouragement that the elder brother was able to give his sister over her reading, are all points of resemblance. The equal terms of the affection of Francis and Jane are of another type.

Henry Tilney and his sister Eleanor, Mrs. Croft and Frederick Wentworth, give us good instances of firm friendships. In the case of the Tilneys, confidences are exchanged with ease and freedom ; but in "Persuasion," the feeling in this respect, as in all others, is more delicate, and only in the chapter which Jane Austen afterwards cancelled can we see the quickness of Mrs. Croft's perceptions where her brother was concerned. For so long as she supposes him to be on the brink of marrying Louisa Musgrove, sympathy is no doubt somewhat difficult to force, but " prompt welcome " is given to Anne as Captain Wentworth's chosen wife ; and with some knowledge of Mrs. Croft we know that the "particularly friendly manner " hid a warmth of feeling which would fully satisfy even Frederick's notions of the love which Anne deserved. But it is in " Mansfield Park " that " brothers and sisters " play the strongest part. No one can possibly doubt the very lively affection of Mary and Henry Crawford. Even when complaining of the

Brothers and Sisters

shortness of his letters, she says that Henry is "exactly what a brother should be, loves me, consults me, confides in me, and will talk to me by the hour together"—and the scene later on, where he tells of his devotion to Fanny Price, is as pretty an account of such a confidence as can be well imagined, where the worldliness of each is almost lost in the happiness of disinterested love, which both are feeling.

When Jane Austen comes to describing Fanny's love for her brother William, her tenderness and her humour are in perfect accord. From the reality of the feelings over his arrival and promotion, to the quiet hit at the enthusiasm which his deserted chair and cold pork bones might be supposed to arouse in Fanny's heart after their early breakfast, when he was off to London, the picture of sisterly love is perfect. We are told, too, that there was "an affection on his side as warm as her own, and much less encumbered by refinement and self-distrust. She was the first object of his love, but it was a love which his stronger spirits and bolder temper made it as natural for him to express as to feel." So far this describes the love of William and Fanny, but a few lines further on comes a passage which has the ring of personal experience. In reading it, it is impossible not to picture a time which was always of great importance in the life at Steventon—the return on leave for a few weeks or a few months of one or other of the sailor brothers, and all the walks and talks which filled up the pleasant days. " On the morrow they were walking about together with true enjoyment, and every succeeding morrow renewed the *tête-à-tête.* Fanny had never known so much felicity in her life as in this unchecked, equal, fearless intercourse with the brother and friend, who was opening all his heart to her, telling her all his hopes and fears, plans and solicitudes respecting that long thought of, dearly earned, and justly valued blessing of promotion—who was interested in all the comforts and all the little hardships of her home—and with whom (perhaps the dearest indulgence of the whole) all the evil and good of their earliest years could be gone over again, and every former united pain and pleasure retraced with the fondest recollection."

Some slight record of the childhood of the Steventon family has been left to us. Most of the known facts have already been told by admirers of Jane Austen, but some extracts from an account written by Catherine Austen in the lifetime of her father, Sir Francis Austen, will at least have the merit of accuracy, for he would certainly have been merciless to even the simplest "embroidery."

The father, Mr. George Austen, was the rector of Steventon. He was known in his young days,

THE REVEREND GEORGE AUSTEN
IN 1763

Brothers and Sisters

before his marriage, as "the handsome tutor," and he transmitted his good looks to at least three of his sons; Henry, Francis, and Charles were all exceptionally handsome men. Indeed, neither wit nor good looks were deficient in the Steventon family. Probably much of Jane's simplicity about her writing arose from the fact that she saw nothing in it to be conceited about, being perfectly convinced that any of the others, with her leisure and inclination, could have done just as well. Her father had a gentleness of disposition combined with a firmness of principle which had great effect in forming the characters of his family. The mother's maiden name was Cassandra Leigh. She was very lively and active, and strict with her children. It is not difficult to see whence Francis derived his ideas of discipline, or Jane her unswerving devotion to duty.

The elder members of the family were born at Deane, which was Mr. Austen's first living, but in 1771 they moved to Steventon, where they lived for nearly thirty years.

The account of the house given by Catherine Austen shows the simplicity of the life.

"The parsonage consisted of three rooms in front on the ground floor, the best parlour, the common parlour, and the kitchen; behind there were Mr. Austen's study, the back kitchen and the stairs; above them were seven bedrooms and three attics. The rooms were low-pitched but not otherwise bad, and compared with the usual style of such buildings it might be considered a very good house." An eulogy follows on the plainness and quietness of the family life—a characteristic specially due to the mother's influence.

"That she had no taste for expensive show or finery, may be inferred from the fact being on record that for two years she actually never had a gown to wear. It was a prevalent custom for ladies to wear cloth habits, and she having one of red cloth found any other dress unnecessary. Imagine a beneficed clergyman's wife in these days contenting herself with such a costume for two years! But the fact illustrates the retired style of living that contented her." Even when she did find it necessary to provide herself with some other costume, the riding-habit was made to serve another useful purpose, for it was cut up into a first cloth suit for little Francis.

The following account of their upbringing closes this slight record :

"There is nothing in which modern manners differ much more from those of a century back than in the system pursued with regard to children. They were kept in the nursery, out of the way not only of visitors but of their parents ; they were trusted to hired attendants ; they were allowed a

Brothers and Sisters

great deal of air and exercise, were kept on plain food, forced to give way to the comfort of others, accustomed to be overlooked, slightly regarded, considered of trifling importance. No well-stocked libraries of varied lore to cheat them into learning awaited them ; no scientific toys, no philosophic amusements enlarged their minds and wearied their attention." One wonders what would have been the verdict of this writer of fifty years ago on education in 1905. She goes on to tell us of the particular system pursued with the boys in order to harden them for their future work in life. It was not considered either necessary or agreeable for a woman to be very strong. "Little Francis was at the age of ten months removed from the parsonage to a cottage in the village, and placed under the care of a worthy couple, whose simple style of living, homely dwelling, and out-of-door habits (for in the country the poor seldom close the door by day, except in bad weather), must have been very different from the heated nurseries and constrained existence of the clean, white-frocked little gentlemen who are now growing up around us. Across the brick floor of a cottage Francis learnt to walk, and perhaps it was here that he received the foundation of the excellent constitution which was so remarkable in after years. It must not, however, be supposed that he was neglected by his parents; he was constantly visited by them both, and often taken to the parsonage."

One cannot but admire the fortitude of parents who would forego the pleasure of seeing their children learn to walk and satisfy themselves with daily visits, for the sake of a plan of education of which the risks cannot have been otherwise than great.

The rough-and-tumble life which followed must have thoroughly suited the taste of any enterprising boy, and given him an independence of spirit, and a habit of making his own plans, which would be exactly what was wanted in the Navy of those days, when a man of twenty-five might be commander of a vessel manned by discontented, almost mutinous, sailors, with the chance of an enemy's ship appearing at any time on the horizon.

Riding about the country after the hounds began for Francis at the age of seven; and, from what we hear of Catherine Morland's childhood, we feel sure that Jane would not always have been contented to be left behind.

Catherine, at the age of ten, was "noisy and wild, hated confinement and cleanliness, and loved nothing so well in the world as rolling down the green slope at the back of the house." When she was fourteen, we are told that she "preferred cricket, base-ball, riding on horseback, and running about the country, to books—or, at least, books of information—for, provided that nothing like useful knowledge could be gained from them, provided they were all story and no reflection, she had never any objection to books at all!"

This, if not an accurate picture of the tastes of the children at Steventon, at least shows the sort of amusements which boys and girls brought up in a country parsonage had at their command.

Perhaps it was of some such recollections that Jane Austen was thinking when she praised that common tie of childish remembrances. "An advantage this, a strengthener of love, in which even the conjugal tie is beneath the fraternal. Children of the same family, the same blood, with the same first association and habits, have some means of enjoyment in their power which no subsequent connection can supply, and it must be by a long and unnatural estrangement, by a divorce which no subsequent connection can justify, if such precious remains of the earliest attachments are ever entirely outlived. Too often, alas! it is so. Fraternal love, sometimes almost everything, is at others worse than nothing. But with William and Fanny Price it was still a sentiment in all its prime and freshness, wounded by no opposition of interest, cooled by no separate attachment, and

Jane Austen's Sailor Brothers

feeling the influence of time and absence only in its increase." That it was never Jane's lot to feel this cooling of affection on the part of any member of her family is due not only to their appreciation of their sister, but to the serenity and adaptability of her own sweet disposition.

CHAPTER II

TWO MIDSHIPMEN

Both Francis and Charles Austen were educated for their profession at the Royal Naval Academy, which was established in 1775 at Portsmouth, and was under the supreme direction of the Lords of the Admiralty. Boys were received there between the ages of 12 and 15. They were supposed to stay there for three years, but there was a system of sending them out to serve on ships as "Volunteers." This was a valuable part of their training, as they were still under the direction of the College authorities, and had the double advantages of experience and of teaching. They did the work of seamen on board, but were allowed up on deck, and were specially under the eye of the captain, who was supposed to make them keep accurate journals, and draw the appearances of headlands and coasts. It is no doubt to this early training that we owe the careful private logs which Francis kept almost throughout his whole career.

Jane Austen's Sailor Brothers

Some of the rules of the Naval Academy show how ideas have altered in the last hundred and more years. There was a special law laid down that masters were to make no differences between the boys on account of rank or position, and no boy was to be allowed to keep a private servant, a rather superfluous regulation in these days.

Three weeks was the extent of the holiday, which it seems could be taken at any time in the year, the Academy being always open for the benefit of Volunteers, who were allowed to go there when their ships were in Portsmouth. Those who distinguished themselves could continue this privilege after their promotion. Francis left the Academy in 1788, and immediately went out to the East Indies on board the *Perseverance* as Volunteer.

There he stayed for four years, first as midshipman on the *Crown*, 64 guns, and afterwards on the *Minerva*, 38.

A very charming letter from his father to Francis is still in existence.

" *Memorandum* for the use of Mr. F. W. Austen on his going to the East Indies on board his Majesty's ship *Perseverance* (Captain Smith).

" December, 1788.

"MY DEAR FRANCIS,—While you were at the Royal Academy the opportunities of writing to you

Two Midshipmen

were so frequent that I gave you my opinion and advice as occasion arose, and it was sufficient to do so ; but now you are going from us for so long a time, and to such a distance, that neither you can consult me or I reply but at long intervals, I think it necessary, therefore, before your departure, to give my sentiments on such general subjects as I conceive of the greatest importance to you, and must leave your conduct in particular cases to be directed by your own good sense and natural judgment of what is right."

After some well-chosen and impressive injunctions on the subject of his son's religious duties, Mr. Austen proceeds :

" Your behaviour, as a member of society, to the individuals around you may be also of great importance to your future well-doing, and certainly will to your present happiness and comfort. You may either by a contemptuous, unkind and selfish manner create disgust and dislike ; or by affability, good humour and compliance, become the object of esteem and affection ; which of these very opposite paths 'tis your interest to pursue I need not say.

" The little world, of which you are going to become an inhabitant, will occasionally have it in their power to contribute no little share to your pleasure or pain ; to conciliate therefore their goodwill, by every honourable method, will be the part of a

prudent man. Your commander and officers will
be most likely to become your friends by a
respectful behaviour to themselves, and by an
active and ready obedience to orders. Good
humour, an inclination to oblige and the carefully avoiding every appearance of selfishness,
will infallibly secure you the regards of your own
mess and of all your equals. With your inferiors
perhaps you will have but little intercourse, but
when it does occur there is a sort of kindness
they have a claim on you for, and which, you
may believe me, will not be thrown away on them.
Your conduct, as it respects yourself, chiefly
comprehends sobriety and prudence. The former
you know the importance of to your health, your
morals and your fortune. I shall therefore say
nothing more to enforce the observance of it. I
thank God you have not at present the least
disposition to deviate from it. Prudence extends
to a variety of objects. Never any action of your
life in which it will not be your interest to consider
what she directs! She will teach you the proper
disposal of your time and the careful management of your money,—two very important trusts
for which you are accountable. She will teach
you that the best chance of rising in life is to make
yourself as useful as possible, by carefully study-
ing everything that relates to your profession,
and distinguishing yourself from those of your

Two Midshipmen

own rank by a superior proficiency in nautical acquirements.

" As you have hitherto, my dear Francis, been extremely fortunate in making friends, I trust your future conduct will confirm their good opinion of you ; and I have the more confidence in this expectation because the high character you acquired at the Academy for propriety of behaviour and diligence in your studies, when you were so much younger and had so much less experience, seems to promise that riper years and more knowledge of the world will strengthen your naturally good disposition. That this may be the case I sincerely pray, as you will readily believe when you are assured that your good mother, brothers, sisters and myself will all exult in your reputation and rejoice in your happiness.

" Thus far by way of general hints for your conduct. I shall now mention only a few particulars I wish your attention to. As you must be convinced it would be the highest satisfaction to us to hear as frequently as possible from you, you will of course neglect no opportunity of giving us that pleasure, and being very minute in what relates to yourself and your situation. On this account, and because unexpected occasions of writing to us may offer, 'twill be a good way always to have a letter in forwardness. You may depend on hearing from some of us at every opportunity.

Jane Austen's Sailor Brothers

"Whenever you draw on me for money, Captain Smith will endorse your bills, and I dare say will readily do it as often, and for what sums, he shall think necessary. At the same time you must not forget to send me the earliest possible notice of the amount of the draft, and the name of the person in whose favour it is drawn. On the subject of letter-writing, I cannot help mentioning how incumbent it is on you to write to Mr. Bayly, both because he desired it and because you have no other way of expressing the sense I know you entertain of his very great kindness and attention to you. Perhaps it would not be amiss if you were also to address one letter to your good friend the commissioner, to acknowledge how much you shall always think yourself obliged to him.

"Keep an exact account of all the money you receive or spend, lend none but where you are sure of an early repayment, and on no account whatever be persuaded to risk it by gaming.

"I have nothing to add but my blessing and best prayers for your health and prosperity, and to beg you would never forget you have not upon earth a more disinterested and warm friend than,

"Your truly affectionate father,

"GEO. AUSTEN."

That this letter should have been found among the private papers of an old man who died at the

Two Midshipmen

age of 91, after a life of constant activity and change, is proof enough that it was highly valued by the boy of fourteen to whom it was written. There is something in its gentleness of tone, and the way in which advice is offered rather than obedience demanded, which would make it very persuasive to the feelings of a young boy going out to a life which must consist mainly of the opposite duties of responsibility and discipline. Incidentally it all throws a pleasant light on the characters of both father and son.

The life of a Volunteer on board ship was by no means an easy one, but it no doubt inured the boys to hardships and privations, and gave them a sympathy with their men which would afterwards stand them in good stead.

The record of Charles as a midshipman is very much more stirring than Francis' experiences. He served on board the *Unicorn*, under Captain Thomas Williams, at the time of the capture of the French frigate *La Tribune*, a notable single ship encounter, which brought Captain Williams the honour of knighthood.

On June 8, 1796, the *Unicorn* and the *Santa Margarita*, cruising off the Scilly Islands, sighted three strange ships, and gave chase. They proved to be two French frigates and a corvette, *La Tribune*, *La Tamise*, and *La Legère*. The French vessels continued all day to run before the wind. The English ships as they gained on them were subjected to a well-directed fire, which kept them back so much that it was evening before *La Tamise* at last bore up and engaged one of the pursuers, the *Santa Margarita*. After a sharp action of about twenty minutes *La Tamise* struck her colours.

La Tribune crowded on all sail to make her escape, but the *Unicorn*, in spite of damage to masts and rigging, kept up the chase, and after a running fight of ten hours the *Unicorn* came alongside, taking the wind from the sails of the French ship. After a close action of thirty-five minutes there was a brief interval. As the smoke cleared away, *La Tribune* could be seen trying to get to the windward of her enemy. This manœuvre was instantly frustrated, and a few more broadsides brought down *La Tribune's* masts, and ended the action. From start to finish of the chase the two vessels had run 210 miles. Not a man was killed or even hurt on board the *Unicorn*, and not a large proportion of the crew of *La Tribune* suffered. No doubt in a running fight of this sort much powder and shot would be expended with very little result.

When this encounter took place Charles Austen had been at sea for scarcely two years. Such an experience would have given the boy a great notion of the excitement and joys in store for him

ACTION BETWEEN THE ENGLISH FRIGATE *UNICORN* AND THE FRENCH FRIGATE *LA TRIBUNE*, JUNE 8, 1796

Two Midshipmen

in a seafaring life. Such, however, was not to
be his luck. Very little important work fell to
his share till at least twenty years later, and for
one of his ardent temperament this was a somewhat hard trial. His day came at last, after
years of routine, but when he was still young
enough to enjoy a life of enterprise and of action.
Even half a century later his characteristic energy
was never more clearly shown than in his last
enterprise as Admiral in command during the
second Burmese War (1852), when he died at the
front.

Francis, during the four years when he was a
midshipman, had only one change of captain.
After serving under Captain Smith in the
Perseverance, he went to the *Crown*, under
Captain the Honourable W. Cornwallis, and
eventually followed him into the *Minerva*.
Admiral Cornwallis was afterwards in command
of the Channel Fleet, blockading Brest in the
Trafalgar year.

Charles had an even better experience than
Francis had, for he was under Captain Thomas
Williams all the time he was midshipman, first
in the *Dædalus*, then in the *Unicorn*, and last in
the *Endymion*.

The fact that both brothers served for nearly
all their times as midshipmen under the same
captain shows that they earned good opinions. If

midshipmen were not satisfactory they were very speedily transferred, as we hear was the lot of poor Dick Musgrave.

" He had been several years at sea, and had in the course of those removals to which all midshipmen are liable, and especially such midshipmen as every captain wishes to get rid of, been six months on board Captain Frederick Wentworth's frigate, the *Laconia ;* and from the *Laconia* he had, under the influence of his captain, written the only two letters which his father and mother had ever received from him during the whole of his absence, that is to say the only two disinterested letters ; all the rest had been mere applications for money. In each letter he had spoken well of his captain—mentioning him in strong, though not perfectly well-spelt praise, as 'a fine dashing felow, only two perticular about the schoolmaster.' "

No doubt Dick's journal and sketches of the coast line were neither accurate nor neatly executed.

William Price's time as a midshipman is, one would think, a nearer approach to the careers of Francis and Charles. Certainly the account given of his talk seems to bear much resemblance to the stories Charles, especially, would have to tell on his return.

" William was often called on by his uncle to

Two Midshipmen

be the talker. His recitals were amusing in themselves to Sir Thomas, but the chief object in
seeking them was to understand the reciter, to
know the young man by his histories, and he
listened to his clear, simple, spirited details with
full satisfaction—seeing in them the proof of good
principles, professional knowledge, energy, courage
and cheerfulness—everything that could deserve
or promise well. Young as he was, William had
already seen a great deal. He had been in the
Mediterranean—in the West Indies—in the
Mediterranean again—had been often taken on
shore by favour of his captain, and in the course
of seven years had known every variety of danger
which sea and war together could offer. With
such means in his power he had a right to be
listened to; and though Mrs. Norris could fidget
about the room, and disturb everybody in quest
of two needlefuls of thread or a second-hand shirt
button in the midst of her nephew's account of a
shipwreck or an engagement, everybody else
was attentive; and even Lady Bertram could
not hear of such horrors unmoved, or without
sometimes lifting her eyes from her work to say,
' Dear me! How disagreeable! I wonder anybody can ever go to sea.'

"To Henry Crawford they gave a different
feeling. He longed to have been at sea, and seen
and done and suffered as much. His heart was

warmed, his fancy fired, and he felt a great respect
for a lad who, before he was twenty, had gone
through such bodily hardships, and given such
proofs of mind. The glory of heroism, of usefulness, of exertion, of endurance, made his own
habits of selfish indulgence appear in shameful
contrast; and he wished he had been a William
Price, distinguishing himself and working his way
to fortune and consequence with so much self-
respect and happy ardour, instead of what he
was!"

This gives a glowing account of the consequence of a midshipman on leave. That times
were not always so good, that they had their
share of feeling small and of no account, on shore
as well as at sea, is only to be expected, and
Fanny was not allowed to imagine anything else.

"'This is the Assembly night,'said William. ' If
I were at Portsmouth, I should be at it perhaps.'

"' But you do not wish yourself at Portsmouth,
William?'

"' No, Fanny, that I do not. I shall have enough
of Portsmouth, and of dancing too, when I cannot
have you. And I do not know that there would
be any good in going to the Assembly, for I might
not get a partner. The Portsmouth girls turn up
their noses at anybody who has not a commission.
One might as well be nothing as a midshipman.
One *is* nothing, indeed. You remember the

Two Midshipmen

Gregorys; they are grown up amazing fine girls, but they will hardly speak to *me*, because Lucy is courted by a lieutenant.'

"'Oh! Shame, shame! But never mind it, William (her own cheeks in a glow of indignation as she spoke). It is not worth minding. It is no reflection on *you;* it is no more than the greatest admirals have all experienced, more or less, in their time. You must think of that; you must try to make up your mind to it as one of the hardships which fall to every sailor's share—like bad weather and hard living—only with this advantage, that there will be an end to it, that there will come a time when you will have nothing of that sort to endure. When you are a lieutenant!—only think, William, when you are a lieutenant, how little you will care for any nonsense of this kind.'"

CHAPTER III

CHANGES AND CHANCES IN THE NAVY

FRANCIS obtained his Lieutenant's commission in 1792, serving for a year in the East Indies, and afterwards on the home station. Early promotions were frequent in those days of the Navy; and, in many ways, no doubt, this custom was a good one, as the younger men had the dash and assurance which was needed, when success lay mainly in the power of making rapid decisions. Very early advancement had nevertheless decided disadvantages, and it was among the causes that brought about the mutinies of 1797. There are four or five cases on record of boys being made captains before they were eighteen, and promotions often went so much by favour and so little by real merit that the discontent of the crews commanded by such inexperienced officers was not at all to be wondered at. There were many other long-standing abuses, not the least of which was the system of punishments, frightful in their severity. A few instances of these, taken

Changes and Chances in the Navy

at haphazard from the logs of the various ships on which Francis Austen served as Lieutenant will illustrate this point.

Glory, December 8, 1795.—"Punished P. C. Smith forty-nine lashes for theft."

January 14, 1796.—"Punished sixteen seamen with one dozen lashes each for neglect of duty in being off the deck in their watch."

Punishments were made as public as possible. The following entry is typical:

Seahorse, December 9, 1797.—"Sent a boat to attend punishments round the fleet."

In the log of the *London*, one of the ships of the line blockading Cadiz, just after the fearful mutinies of 1797, we find, as might be expected, that punishments were more severe than ever.

August 16, 1798.—"*Marlborough* made the signal for punishment. Sent three boats manned and armed to attend the punishment of Charles Moore (seaman belonging to the *Marlborough*), who was sentenced to receive one hundred lashes for insolence to his superior officer. Read the articles of war and sentence of Court-martial to the ship's company. The prisoner received twenty-five lashes alongside this ship."

In the case of a midshipman court-martialled for robbing a Portuguese boat, "the charges having been proved, he was sentenced to be turned before the mast, to have his uniform stripped off him on the quarter-deck before all the ship's company, to have his head shaved, and to be rendered for ever incapable of serving as a petty officer."

No fewer than six executions are recorded in the log of the *London* as taking place among the ships of the fleet off Cadiz. Only one instance is mentioned where the offender was pardoned by the commander-in-chief on account of previous good conduct. Earl St. Vincent certainly deserved his reputation as a disciplinarian.

When, in addition to the system of punishment, it is further considered that the food was almost always rough and very often uneatable, that most of the crews were pressed men, who would rather have been at any other work, and that the seamen's share in any possible prizes was ludicrously small, one wonders, not at the mutinies, but at the splendid loyalty shown when meeting the enemy.

It is a noticeable fact that discontent was rife during long times of inaction (whilst blockading Cadiz is the notable instance), but when it came to fighting for their country men and officers alike managed to forget their grievances.

On May 29, the log of the *London* is as follows :

"The *Marlborough* anchored in the middle of the line. At seven the *Marlborough* made the signal for punishment. Sent our launch, barge and cutter, manned and armed, to attend the execution of Peter Anderson, belonging to the

Changes and Chances in the Navy

Marlborough, who was sentenced to suffer death for mutiny. Read the sentence of the court-martial, and the articles of war to the ship's company. At nine the execution took place." This is a record of an eye-witness of the historic scene which put a stop to organised mutiny in the Cadiz fleet.

The narrative has been often told. Lord St. Vincent's order to the crew of the *Marlborough* that they alone should execute their comrade, the leader of the mutiny—the ship moored at a central point, and surrounded by all the men-of-war's boats armed with carronades under the charge of expert gunners—the *Marlborough's* own guns housed and secured, and ports lowered—every precaution adopted in case of resistance to the Admiral's orders—and the result, in the words of the commander-in-chief: "Discipline is preserved."

Perhaps the relief felt in the fleet was expressed in some measure by the salute of seventeen guns recorded on the same day, "being the anniversary of King Charles' restoration."

Gradually matters were righted. Very early promotions were abolished, and throughout the Navy efforts were made on the part of the officers to make their men more comfortable, and especially to give them better and more wholesome food—but reforms must always be slow if they are

Jane Austen's Sailor Brothers

to do good and not harm, and, necessarily, the lightening of punishments which seem to us barbarous was the slowest of all.

The work of the pressgang is always a subject of some interest and romance. It is difficult to realise that it was a properly authorised Government measure. There were certain limits in which it might work, certain laws to be obeyed. The most useful men, those who were already at sea, but not in the King's service, could not legally be impressed, unless they were free from all former obligations, and the same rule applied to apprentices. These rules were not, however, strictly kept, and much trouble was often caused by the wrong men being impressed, or by false statements being used to get others off. The following letter, written much later in his career by Francis Austen when he was Captain of the *Leopard* in 1804, gives a typical case of this kind.

Leopard, DUNGENESS, August 10, 1804.

"SIR,—I have to acknowledge the receipt of your letter of the 17th inst., with the enclosure, relative to Harris Walker, said to be chief mate of the *Fanny*, and in reply thereto have the honour to inform you that the said Harris Walker was impressed from on board the brig *Fanny*, off Dungeness, by Lieutenant Taylor of his Majesty's ship under my command, on the evening of the

Changes and Chances in the Navy

7th inst., because no documents proving him to be actually chief mate of the brig were produced, and because the account he gave of himself was unsatisfactory and contradictory. On examining him the following day he at first confessed to me that he had entered on board the *Fanny* only three days before she sailed from Tobago, in consequence of the captain (a relation of his) being taken ill, and shortly afterwards he asserted that the whole of the cargo had been taken on board and stowed under his direction. The master of the *Fanny* told Lieutenant Taylor that his cargo had been shipped more than a fortnight before he sailed, having been detained for want of a copy of the ship's register, she being a prize purchased and fitted at Tobago. From these very contradictory accounts—from the man's having no affidavit to produce of his being actual chief mate of the brig, from his not having signed any articles as such—and from his handwriting totally disagreeing with the Log-Book (said to have been kept by himself) I felt myself perfectly justified in detaining him for his Majesty's service.

" I return the enclosure, and have the honour to be,

"Sir, your obedient humble servant,

"FRANCIS WM. AUSTEN.

"Thomas Louis, Esq.,

"Rear-Admiral of the Blue."

Jane Austen's Sailor Brothers

The reason assigned, that the reports Harris Walker gave of himself were "unsatisfactory and contradictory," seems to us a bad one for "detaining him for his Majesty's service," but it shows clearly how great were the difficulties in keeping up the supply of men. Captain Austen had not heard the last of this man, as the belief seems to have been strong that he was not legally impressed. Harris Walker, however, settled the matter by deserting on October 5.

An entry in the log of the newly built frigate *Triton*, under Captain Gore, gives an instance of wholesale, and one would think entirely illegal action.

November 25, 1796, in the Thames (Long Reach).

"Sent all the boats to impress the crew of the *Britannia* East India ship. The boats returned with thirty-nine men, the remainder having armed themselves and barricaded the bread room."

"26th, the remainder of the *Britannia* crew surrendered, being twenty-three. Brought them on board."

So great was the necessity of getting more men, and a better stamp of men, into the Navy, and of making them fairly content when there, that in 1800 a Royal Proclamation was issued encouraging men to enlist, and promising them a bounty.

Changes and Chances in the Navy

This bounty, though it worked well in many cases, was of course open to various forms of abuse. Some who were entitled to it did not get it, and many put in a claim whose right was at least doubtful. An instance appears in the letters of the *Leopard* of a certain George Rivers, who had been entered as a "prest man," and applied successfully to be considered as a Volunteer, thereby to procure the bounty. He evidently wanted to make the best of his position.

The case of Thomas Roberts, given in another letter from the *Leopard*, is an example of inducements offered to enter the service.

Thomas Roberts "appears to have been received as a Volunteer from H.M.S. *Ceres*, and received thirty shillings bounty. He says he was apprenticed to his father about three years ago, and that, sometime last October, he was enticed to a public-house by two men, who afterwards took him on board the receiving ship off the Tower, where he was persuaded to enter the service."

The difficulty of getting an adequate crew seems to have led in some cases to sharp practice among the officers themselves, if we are to believe that Admiral Croft had real cause for complaint.

"'If you look across the street,' he says to Anne Elliot, 'you will see Admiral Brand coming down, and his brother. Shabby fellows, both of them! I am glad they are not on this side of the

way. Sophy cannot bear them. They played me
a pitiful trick once ; got away some of my best
men. I will tell you the whole story another
time.'" But "another time" never comes, so we
are reduced to imagining the "pitiful trick."

The unpopularity of the Navy, and the consequent shorthandedness in time of war, had one
very bad result in bringing into it all sorts of
undesirable foreigners, who stirred up strife
among the better disposed men, and altogether
aggravated the evils of the service.

Undoubtedly the care of the officers for their
men was doing its gradual work in lessening all
these evils. To instance this, we find, as we read
on in the letters and official reports of Francis
Austen, that the entry, "the man named in the
margin did run from his Majesty's ship under my
command," comes with less and less frequency ;
and we have on record that the *Aurora*, under the
command of Captain Charles Austen, did not lose
a single man by sickness or desertion during the
years 1826–1828, whilst he was in command.
Even when some allowance is made for his
undoubted charm of personality, this is a strong
evidence of the real improvements which had been
worked in the Navy during thirty years.

With such constant difficulties and discomforts
to contend with, it seems in some ways remarkable that the Navy should have been so popular as

Changes and Chances in the Navy

a profession among the classes from which officers were drawn. Some of this popularity, and no doubt a large share, was the effect of a strong feeling of patriotism, and some was due to the fact that the Navy was a profession in which it was possible to get on very fast. A man of moderate luck and enterprise was sure to make some sort of mark, and if to this he added any "interest" his success was assured. Success, in those days of the Navy, meant money. It is difficult for us to realise the large part played by "prizes" in the ordinary routine work of the smallest sloop. In the case of Captain Wentworth, a very fair average instance, we know that when he engaged himself to Anne Elliot, he had "nothing but himself to recommend him, no hopes of attaining influence, but in the chances of a most uncertain profession, and no connexions to secure even his farther rise in that profession," yet we find that his hopes for his own advancement were fully justified. Jane Austen would have been very sure to have heard of it from Francis if not from Charles, if she had made Captain Wentworth's success much more remarkable than that of the ordinary run of men in such circumstances.

We are clearly told what those circumstances were.

"Captain Wentworth had no fortune. He had been lucky in his profession ; but spending freely what had come freely had realised nothing. But he was confident that he would soon be rich ; full of life and ardour, he knew that he would soon have a ship, and soon be on a station that would lead to everything he wanted. He had always been lucky ; he knew he should be so still." Later, " all his sanguine expectations, all his confidence had been justified. His genius and ardour had seemed to foresee and to command his prosperous path. He had, very soon after their engagement ceased, got employ ; and all that he had told her would follow had taken place. He had distinguished himself, and early gained the other step in rank, and must now, by successive captures, have made a handsome fortune. She had only Navy Lists and newspapers for her authority, but she could not doubt his being rich."

Such were some of the inducements. That " Jack ashore " was a much beloved person may also have had its influence. Anne Elliot speaks for the greater part of the nation when she says, " the Navy, I think, who have done so much for us, have at least an equal claim with any other set of men, for all the comforts and all the privileges which any home can give. Sailors work hard enough for their comforts we must allow."

That Sir Walter Elliot represents another large section of the community is, however, not to be

Changes and Chances in the Navy

denied, but his opinions are not of the sort to act as a deterrent to any young man bent on following a gallant profession.

"Sir Walter's remark was : 'The profession has its utility, but I should be sorry to see any friend of mine belonging to it."

"'Indeed!' was the reply, and with a look of surprise.

"'Yes, it is in two points offensive to me; I have two strong grounds of objection to it. First, as being the means of bringing persons of obscure birth into undue distinction, and raising men to honours which their fathers and grand-fathers never dreamt of; and, secondly, as it cuts up a man's youth and vigour most horribly; a sailor grows old sooner than any other man. I have observed it all my life. A man is in greater danger in the Navy of being insulted by the rise of one whose father his father might have disdained to speak to, and of becoming prematurely an object of disgust to himself, than in any other line. One day last spring in town I was in company with two men, striking instances of what I am talking of : Lord St. Ives, whose father we all know to have been a country curate, without bread to eat : I was to give place to Lord St. Ives, and a certain Admiral Baldwin, the most deplorable-looking personage you can imagine; his face the colour of mahogany, rough and rugged to the last

Jane Austen's Sailor Brothers

degree; all lines and wrinkles, nine grey hairs of a side, and nothing but a dab of powder at top.'

" ' In the name of heaven, who is that old fellow?' said I to a friend of mine who was standing near (Sir Basil Morley), ' Old fellow!' cried Sir Basil, ' it is Admiral Baldwin.'

" ' What do you take his age to be?'

" ' Sixty,' said I, ' or perhaps sixty-two.'

" ' Forty,' replied Sir Basil, ' forty, and no more.'

" ' Picture to yourselves my amazement. I shall not easily forget Admiral Baldwin. I never saw quite so wretched an example of what a seafaring life can do; they all are knocked about, and exposed to every climate and every weather till they are not fit to be seen. It is a pity they are not knocked on the head at once, before they reach Admiral Baldwin's age.' "

CHAPTER IV

PROMOTIONS

As Lieutenant, Francis Austen had very different experience and surroundings to those of his days as a midshipman. For three years and more he was in various ships on the home station, which meant a constant round of dull routine work, enlivened only by chances of getting home for a few days. While serving in the *Lark* sloop, he accompanied to Cuxhaven the squadron told off to bring to England Princess Caroline of Brunswick, soon to become Princess of Wales. The voyage out seems to have been arctic in its severity. This bad weather, combined with dense fogs, caused the *Lark* to get separated from the rest of the squadron, and from March 6 till the 11th nothing was seen or heard of the sloop. On March 18 the Princess came on board the *Jupiter*, the flagship of the squadron, and arrived in England on April 5 after a fair passage, but a voyage about as long as that to the Cape of Good Hope nowadays.

Jane Austen's Sailor Brothers

Francis notes in the log of the *Glory*, that while cruising, "the *Rattler* cutter joined company, and informed us she yesterday spoke H.M.S. *Dædalus*"—a matter of some interest to him, as Charles was then on board the *Dædalus* as midshipman, under Captain Thomas Williams. Captain Williams had married Jane Cooper, a cousin of Jane Austen, who was inclined to tease him about his having "no taste in names." The following extract from one of her letters to Cassandra touches on nearly all these facts :

"SUNDAY, *January* 10, 1796.

" By not returning till the 19th, you will exactly contrive to miss seeing the Coopers, which I suppose it is your wish to do. We have heard nothing from Charles for some time. One would suppose they must have sailed by this time, as the wind is so favourable. What a funny name Tom has got for his vessel! But he has no taste in names, as we well know, and I dare say he christened it himself."

Tom seems to have been a great favourite with his wife's cousins. Only a few days later Jane writes :

" How impertinent you are to write to me about Tom, as if I had not opportunities of hearing from him myself. The *last* letter I received from him

Promotions

was dated on Friday the 8th, and he told me that if the wind should be favourable on Sunday, which it proved to be, they were to sail from Falmouth on that day. By this time, therefore, they are at Barbadoes, I suppose."

Having the two brothers constantly backwards and forwards must have been very pleasant at Steventon. Almost every letter has some reference to one or the other.

" Edward and Frank are both gone forth to seek their fortunes ; the latter is to return soon and help us to seek ours."

Later from Rowling, Edward Austen's home, she writes :

" If this scheme holds, I shall hardly be at Steventon before the middle of the month ; but if you cannot do without me I could return, I suppose, with Frank, if he ever goes back. He enjoys himself here very much, for he has just learnt to turn, and is so delighted with the employment that he is at it all day long. . . . What a fine fellow Charles is, to deceive us into writing two letters to him at Cork ! I admire his ingenuity extremely, especially as he is so great a gainer by it. . . . Frank has turned a very nice little butter-churn for Fanny. . . . We walked Frank last night to (church at) Crixhall Ruff, and he appeared much edified. So his Royal Highness Sir Thomas Williams has at length sailed ; the papers say ' on a cruise.'

Jane Austen's Sailor Brothers

But I hope they are gone to Cork, or I shall have written in vain. . . . Edward and Fly (short for Frank) went out yesterday very early in a couple of shooting-jackets, and came home like a couple of bad shots, for they killed nothing at all.

" They are out again to-day, and are not yet returned. Delightful sport! They are just come home—Edward with his two brace, Frank with his two and a half. What amiable young men ! "

About the middle of September 1796 Frank was appointed to the *Triton*, which event is announced to Cassandra in these terms :

" This morning has been spent in doubt and deliberation, forming plans and removing difficulties, for it ushered in the day with an event which I had not intended should take place so soon by a week. Frank has received his appointment on board the *Captain John Gore*, commanded by the *Triton*, and will therefore be obliged to be in town on Wednesday ; and though I have every disposition in the world to accompany him on that day, I cannot go on the uncertainty of the Pearsons being at home.

" The *Triton* is a new 32-frigate, just launched at Deptford. Frank is much pleased with the prospect of having Captain Gore under his command."

Francis stayed on board the *Triton* for about eighteen months. He then spent six months in

FRANCIS AUSTEN IN 1796

Promotions

the *Seahorse* before his appointment to the *London*
off Cadiz, in February 1798. On April 30 following is recorded in the log of the *London* the arrival of H.M.S. *Vanguard*, carrying Rear-Admiral
Sir Horatio Nelson's flag, and on May 3 the
Vanguard proceeded to Gibraltar. On May 24
the "detached squadron" sailed as follows: *Culloden* (Captain Troubridge), *Bellerophon, Defence,
Theseus, Goliath, Zealous, Minotaur, Majestic*, and
Swiftsure.

These three entries foreshadow the Battle of the
Nile, on August 1. The account of this victory
was read to the crew of the *London* on September
27, and on October 24 they "saw eleven sail in
the south-west—the *Orion* and the French line of
battleships, prizes to Admiral Sir Horatio Nelson's
fleet."

Now and then the *London* went as far as Ceuta
or Gibraltar, and the log notes, "Cape Trafalgar
East 7 leagues."

It is curious to think that "Trafalgar" conveyed
nothing remarkable to the writer. One wonders
too what view would have been expressed as to
the plan of making Gibraltar a naval command,
obviously advantageous in twentieth-century conditions, but probably open to many objections in
those days.

Charles, in December 1797, was promoted to
be a Lieutenant, serving in the *Scorpion*. There

45

Jane Austen's Sailor Brothers

is something in the account of William Price's joy
over his promotion which irresistibly calls up the
picture of Charles in the same circumstances.
Francis would always have carried his honours
with decorum, but Charles' bubbling enthusiasm
would have been more difficult to restrain.

"William had obtained a ten days' leave of
absence, to be given to Northamptonshire, and
was coming to show his happiness and describe
his uniform. He came, and he would have been
delighted to show his uniform there too, had not
cruel custom prohibited its appearance except on
duty. So the uniform remained at Portsmouth,
and Edmund conjectured that before Fanny had
any chance of seeing it, all its own freshness, and
all the freshness of its wearer's feelings, must be
worn away. It would be sunk into a badge of
disgrace; for what can be more unbecoming or
more worthless than the uniform of a lieutenant
who has been a lieutenant a year or two, and sees
others made commanders before him? So
reasoned Edmund, till his father made him the
confidant of a scheme which placed Fanny's
chance of seeing the Second Lieutenant of
H.M.S. *Thrush* in all his glory, in another light.
This scheme was that she should accompany her
brother back to Portsmouth, and spend a little
time with her own family. William was almost
as happy in the plan as his sister. It would be

Promotions

the greatest pleasure to him to have her there to
the last moment before he sailed, and perhaps find
her there still when he came in from his first
cruise. And, besides, he wanted her so very much
to see the *Thrush* before she went out of harbour
(the *Thrush* was certainly the finest sloop in the
service). And there were several improvements
in the dockyard, too, which he quite longed to show
her. . . . Of pleasant talk between the brother
and sister there was no end. Everything supplied
an amusement to the high glee of William's mind,
and he was full of frolic and joke in the intervals
of their high-toned subjects, all of which ended,
if they did not begin, in praise of the *Thrush*—
conjectures how she would be employed, schemes
for an action with some superior force, which (sup-
posing the first lieutenant out of the way—and
William was not very merciful to the first lieutenant) was to give himself the next step as soon
as possible, or speculations upon prize-money,
which was to be generously distributed at home
with only the reservation of enough to make the
little cottage comfortable in which he and Fanny
were to pass all their middle and later life together."

Charles's year in the *Scorpion* was spent under
the command of Captain John Tremayne Rodd.
The chief event was the capture of the *Courier*,
a Dutch brig carrying six guns. Undoubtedly the

life was dull on a small brig, and Charles as midshipman had not been used to be dull. He evidently soon began to be restless, and to agitate for removal, which he got just about the same time as that of Francis's promotion.

In December 1798 Francis was made Commander of the *Peterel* sloop, and Charles, still as Lieutenant, was moved from the *Scorpion* to the frigate *Tamar*, and eventually to the *Endymion*, commanded by his old friend and captain, Sir Thomas Williams.

Charles had evidently written to his sister Cassandra to complain of his hard lot. Cassandra was away at the time, staying with Edward Austen at Godmersham, but she sent the letter home, and on December 18 Jane writes in answer :

" I am sorry our dear Charles begins to feel the dignity of ill-usage. My father will write to Admiral Gambier " (who was then one of the Lords of the Admiralty). " He must have already received so much satisfaction from his acquaintance and patronage of Frank, that he will be delighted, I dare say, to have another of the family introduced to him. I think it would be very right in Charles to address Sir Thomas on the occasion, though I cannot approve of your scheme of writing to him (which you communicated to me a few nights ago) to request him to come home and convey you to Steventon. To do you justice,

Promotions

you had some doubts of the propriety of such a measure yourself. The letter to Gambier goes to-day."

This is followed, on December 24, by a letter which must have been as delightful to write as to receive.

"I have got some pleasant news for you which I am eager to communicate, and therefore begin my letter sooner, though I shall not send it sooner than usual. Admiral Gambier, in reply to my father's application, writes as follows: 'As it is usual to keep young officers' (Charles was then only nineteen) 'in small vessels, it being most proper on account of their inexperience, and it being also a situation where they are more in the way of learning their duty, your son has been continued in the *Scorpion*; but I have mentioned to the Board of Admiralty his wish to be in a frigate, and when a proper opportunity offers, and it is judged that he has taken his turn in a small ship, I hope he will be removed. With regard to your son now in the *London*, I am glad I can give you the assurance that his promotion is likely to take place very soon, as Lord Spencer has been so good as to say he would include him in an arrangement that he proposes making in a short time relative to some promotions in that quarter.'

"There! I may now finish my letter and go

and hang myself, for I am sure I can neither write nor do anything which will not appear insipid to you after this. Now I really think he will soon be made, and only wish we could communicate our foreknowledge of the event to him whom it principally concerns. My father has written to Daysh to desire that he will inform us, if he can, when the commission is sent. Your chief wish is now ready to be accomplished, and could Lord Spencer give happiness to Martha at the same time, what a joyful heart he would make of yours!"

It is quite clear from this, and many other of the letters of Jane to Cassandra, that both sisters were anxious to bring off a match between Frank and their great friend, Martha Lloyd, whose younger sister was the wife of James Austen. Martha Lloyd eventually became Frank's second wife nearly thirty years after the date of this letter.

Jane continues her letter by saying:

" I have sent the same extract of the sweets of Gambier to Charles, who, poor fellow! though he sinks into nothing but an humble attendant on the hero of the piece, will, I hope, be contented with the prospect held out to him. By what the Admiral says, it appears as if he had been designedly kept in the *Scorpion*. But I will not torment myself with conjectures and suppositions. Facts

Promotions

shall satisfy me. Frank had not heard from any of us for ten weeks, when he wrote to me on November 12, in consequence of Lord St. Vincent being removed to Gibraltar. When his commission is sent, however, it will not be so long on its road as our letters, because all the Government despatches are forwarded by land to his lordship from Lisbon with great regularity. The lords of the Admiralty will have enough of our applications at present, for I hear from Charles that he has written to Lord Spencer himself to be removed. I am afraid his Serene Highness will be in a passion, and order some of our heads to be cut off."

The next letter, of December 28, is the culminating-point:

"Frank is made. He was yesterday raised to the rank of Commander, and appointed to the *Peterel* sloop, now at Gibraltar. A letter from Daysh has just announced this, and as it is confirmed by a very friendly one from Mr. Matthew to the same effect, transcribing one from Admiral Gambier to the General, we have no reason to suspect the truth of it.

"As soon as you have cried a little for joy, you may go on, and learn farther that the India House have taken Captain Austen's petition into consideration—this comes from Daysh—and likewise that Lieutenant Charles John Austen is removed to the *Tamar* frigate—this comes from the Admiral. We cannot find out where the *Tamar* is, but I hope we shall now see Charles here at all events.

"This letter is to be dedicated entirely to good news. If you will send my father an account of your washing and letter expenses, &c., he will send you a draft for the amount of it, as well as for your next quarter, and for Edward's rent. If you don't buy a muslin gown on the strength of this money and Frank's promotion I shall never forgive you.

"Mrs. Lefroy has just sent me word that Lady Dorchester meant to invite me to her ball on January 8, which, though an humble blessing compared with what the last page records, I do not consider any calamity. I cannot write any more now, but I have written enough to make you very happy, and therefore may safely conclude."

Jane was in great hopes that Charles would get home in time for this ball at Kempshot, but he "could not get superceded in time," and so did not arrive until some days later. On January 21 we find him going off to join his ship, not very well pleased with existing arrangements.

"Charles leaves us to-night. The *Tamar* is in the Downs, and Mr. Daysh advises him to join her there directly, as there is no chance of her going to the westward. Charles does not approve

Promotions

of this at all, and will not be much grieved if he should be too late for her before she sails, as he may then hope to get a better station. He attempted to go to town last night, and got as far on his road thither as Dean Gate; but both the coaches were full, and we had the pleasure of seeing him back again. He will call on Daysh to-morrow, to know whether the *Tamar* has sailed or not, and if she is still at the Downs he will proceed in one of the night coaches to Deal.

" I want to go with him, that I may explain the country properly to him between Canterbury and Rowling, but the unpleasantness of returning by myself deters me. I should like to go as far as Ospringe with him very much indeed, that I might surprise you at Godmersham."

Charles evidently did get off this time, for we read a few days later that he had written from the Downs, and was pleased to find himself Second Lieutenant on board the *Tamar*.

The *Endymion* was also in the Downs, a further cause of satisfaction. It was only three weeks later that Charles was reappointed to the *Endymion* as Lieutenant, in which frigate he saw much service. chiefly off Algeciras, under his old friend " Tom." One is inclined to wonder how far this accidental meeting in the Downs influenced the appointment. Charles appears on many occasions to have had a quite remarkable gift for getting what he wanted.

Jane Austen's Sailor Brothers

His charm of manner, handsome face, and affectionate disposition, combined with untiring enthusiasm, must have made him very hard to resist, and he evidently had no scruple about making his wants clear to all whom it might concern. The exact value of interest in these matters is always difficult to gauge, but there is no doubt that a well-timed application was nearly always necessary for advancement. The account of the way in which Henry Crawford secured promotion for William Price is no doubt an excellent example of how things were done.

Henry takes William to dinner with the Admiral, and encourages him to talk. The Admiral takes a fancy to the young man, and speaks to some friends about him with a view to his promotion. The result is contained in the letters which Henry so joyfully hands over to Fanny to read.

" Fanny could not speak, but he did not want her to speak. To see the expression of her eyes, the change of her complexion, the progress of her feelings—their doubt, confusion and felicity—was enough. She took the letters as he gave them. The first was from the Admiral to inform his nephew, in a few words, of his having succeeded in the object he had undertaken (the promotion of young Price), and enclosing two more—one from the secretary of the First Lord to a friend, whom the Admiral had set to work in the business ;

Promotions

the other from that friend to himself, by which it appeared that his lordship had the very great happiness of attending to the recommendation of Sir Charles ; that Sir Charles was much delighted in having such an opportunity of proving his regard for Admiral Crawford, and that the circumstances of Mr. William Price's commission as Second Lieutenant of H.M. sloop *Thrush* being made out, was spreading general joy through a wide circle of great people."

CHAPTER V

THE *PETEREL* SLOOP

IT will, perhaps, be as well to recall some of the principal events of the war, during the few years before Francis took up his command of the *Peterel*, in order that his work may be better understood.

Spain had allied herself with France in 1796, and early in the following year matters looked most unpromising for England. The British fleet had been obliged to leave the Mediterranean. Bonaparte was gaining successes against Austria on land. The peace negotiations, which had been begun by France, had been peremptorily stopped, while the French expedition to Ireland obviously owed its failure to bad weather, and not in the least to any effective interference on the part of the British Navy. Altogether the horizon was dark, and every one in England was expecting to hear of crushing disaster dealt out by the combined fleets of France and Spain, and all lived in fear of invasion. Very different was the

The *Peterel* Sloop

news that arrived in London early in March. Sir
John Jervis, with Nelson and Collingwood, met
the Spanish fleet off Cape St. Vincent on
Valentine's Day, and we all know the result. As
Jervis said on the morning of the fight, " A victory
was essential to England at this moment." The
confidence of the nation returned, and was not
lost again through the hard struggle of the following years. An extract from the log of Lieutenant
F. W. Austen, on board the frigate *Seahorse*, in
the Hamoaze, October 6, 1797, reads as follows :
" Came into harbour the *San Josef, Salvador del
Mundo, San Nicolai*, and *San Isidore*, Spanish
line-of-battle ships, captured by the fleet under
Lord St. Vincent on the 14th February."

After their defeat, the remainder of the Spanish
fleet entered the port of Cadiz, and were for the
next two years blockaded by Admiral Jervis, now
Earl St. Vincent. In this blockade, Francis
Austen took part, serving in the *London.*

During this time of comparative inaction, the
fearful mutinies, described in a former chapter,
seemed to be sapping the strength of the Navy.
The greater number of the British ships were
concentrated in the Channel under Lord Bridport,
and were employed in watching the harbour of
Brest, in order to prevent the French fleet from
escaping, with what success we shall presently
tell. Our flag was scarcely to be seen inside the

Jane Austen's Sailor Brothers

Mediterranean except on a few sloops of war.
Each side was waiting for some movement of
aggression from the other. Now was Bonaparte's
chance to get to the East. His plans were quietly
and secretly formed. An armament was prepared
at Toulon almost unknown to the British, and at
the same time all possible measures to avert sus-
picion were taken. The Spanish fleet in Cadiz
formed up as if for departure, and so kept Lord St.
Vincent on the watch, while Bonaparte himself
stayed in Paris until the expedition was quite ready
to start, in order to give the idea that the invasion
of England was intended. Still it was not practicable to keep the preparations entirely secret
for any length of time.

Early in April 1798 Nelson sailed from
England, joined St. Vincent at Cadiz, and immediately went on into the Mediterranean, with three
ships of the line, to reconnoitre. He was reinforced by nine more under Troubridge, and Lord
St. Vincent had orders from home to follow with
the entire squadron if it should prove necessary.
Nelson searched for Bonaparte in the Mediterranean, and missed him twice. The French
seized Malta for the sake of getting their supplies
through, but the British as promptly blockaded it.
At last, on August 1, Nelson came upon the
French fleet anchored in Aboukir Bay, and the
Battle of the Nile was fought. The situation

The *Peterel* Sloop

now created can be briefly summarised. Bonaparte was in Egypt, cut off from all communication with France, and however determinedly he might turn his face towards Africa or Asia his position was a serious one. Turkey almost immediately declared war against France. Malta was still closely blockaded by the British. Nelson had established himself at Palermo, on friendly terms with the King of Naples, who had taken refuge in Sicily. The news of the Battle of the Nile had spread far and wide, and France had good reason to fear that the tide had turned against her.

Early in 1799 Bonaparte attacked Acre, and Sir Sydney Smith was sent to harass his forces, and to compel him, if possible, to raise the siege.

At this time occurred one of those events which show how a slight advantage, properly used, may decide the final issue. Matters were in this critical state; every British ship in and near the Mediterranean was employed at some important work, when that happened which might have been the cause of serious disaster. Admiral Bruix got away from Brest with a fleet of twenty-five sail of the line and ten smaller ships.

The blame of this mishap is not at all easy to attach. Lord Bridport was still in command of the Channel Fleet, but the Admiralty seemed to prefer to keep him in touch with headquarters off the coast of Kent, rather than to allow him to maintain a position whence he could more easily keep watch on the French fleet. Now ensued an exciting time. No one knew where the French fleet was, much less whither it was bound. They had escaped in a thick fog, being seen only by *La Nymphe*, one of the British frigates, whose officers, owing to the density of the fog, imagined that they saw the fleet bring to under the land, and signalled accordingly to Lord Bridport. When the fog lifted the French fleet was no longer in sight.

Of course the first idea was that they had gone to Ireland, and off went Lord Bridport to pursue them. A little later news was received that they had sailed southward, and a correspondent at this time writes: "Lord St. Vincent will have a fine field to exert his talents if the French fleet join the Spanish, after capturing Lisbon."

On the morning of May 5, from the Rock of Gibraltar, Lord St. Vincent saw, with the deepest anxiety, the French fleet running before a westerly gale into the Mediterranean. His most immediate fear was lest Bruix should be on his way to help Bonaparte at Acre, and to overwhelm Sydney Smith's squadron. If so, the question was how to stop him. Lord Bridport's fleet was useless, as it was not until nearly four weeks later that he was able to send help. Lord Keith was

The *Peterel* Sloop

blockading Cadiz. If he left, the whole Spanish fleet would be released and at liberty to attack where they would. Nelson was at Palermo with only one British line-of-battle ship, and great would be the consternation in the town if that one ship were to be withdrawn. A small squadron was blockading Malta, and a few ships were at Minorca under Commodore Duckworth, but Port Mahon was not yet fully garrisoned. Troubridge was outside Naples. Bruix might attack any of these divisions with the full force of his fleet, or he might proceed straight to Egypt. St. Vincent had to determine which of these positions should be abandoned in order to meet the French fleet. He decided on ordering Keith into the Mediterranean so as to concentrate the available forces, sending word as far as possible to the outlying squadrons.

To Nelson at Palermo he wrote that he expected the enemy to proceed to Malta and Alexandria. This despatch was entrusted to the *Hyena*, which fell in with the *Peterel*, now under the command of Francis Austen. The *Peterel* was already on the way to Nelson with a despatch from Minorca, and, being a fast-sailing sloop, the captain of the *Hyena* at once handed on the important paper to be delivered by Captain Austen.

The entries in the log of the *Peterel* at this date tell their own story :

Jane Austen's Sailor Brothers

"*May* 10.—On the passage from Minorca to Palermo.

"12 noon.—Off shore four or five miles.

"2 o'clock.—Answered the private signal made by a ship in the S.S.E.

"4 o'clock.—Showed our pendants to a ship in the S.S.E.

"5 o'clock.—Joined H.M.S. *Hyena ;* lowered the jolly-boat, and went on board.

"10 past 5.—Up boat and made all sail ; the *Hyena* parted company, standing to the N.W.

"*May* 12. A quarter past 9.—Saw a sail on the lee bow, made the private signal to her, which was answered. Made the signal for having gained intelligence, and repeated it with four guns, but it was not answered.

"15 minutes past 11.—Hove to ; lowered the jolly-boat and went on board the stranger, which proved to be H.M.S. *Pallas*, with a convoy for the westward.

"20 minutes past 11.—Up boat, filled, and made all sail as before. Observed the *Pallas* bear up and follow us with her convoy.

"*May* 13.—At daylight, Cape Trepano (in Sicily). S.S.W. five or six leagues.

"A quarter-past 3 P.M.—Shortened sail, backed ship, hove to and lowered the boat. The first lieutenant went on shore with despatches for Lord Nelson at Palermo.

The *Peterel* Sloop

"A quarter before 4.—The boat returned, hoisted her up, and made all sail.

"NOTE.—The place at which the first lieutenant landed was on the east side of the Bay, between Cape St. Vito and Cape Alos, and about twenty-four miles by road from Palermo."

The following is the letter which Captain Austen sent to the Admiral, with the despatches :

"*Peterel* AT SEA, OFF CAPE ST. VITO, *May* 13, 1799.

"MY LORD,—I have the honour to inform your Lordship that I sailed from the Island of Minorca with his Majesty's sloop under my command, at 11 A.M. on Friday, the 10th inst., charged with the accompanying despatch for your lordship, and the same evening met his Majesty's ship *Hyena*, about five leagues S.E. by S. of Fort Mahon, from the captain of which I received the paper enclosed ; and judging from the contents of it that its speedy arrival must be of the utmost consequence, and that a passage by land may be performed in much less time than by sea, with the wind as it now is at the E.S.E., I have directed Mr. Staines, my first lieutenant, to land with the despatch at Castella, and proceed with all possible expedition to your lordship at Palermo, to which place I shall carry his Majesty's sloop as soon as I can.

"I fell in with his Majesty s ship *Pallas* and

convoy yesterday at 11 A.M., about fifteen leagues E.S.E. of Cape Carbonera, and, in consequence of the intelligence I gave the captain of that ship bore up with his convoy for Palermo. I enclose the state and condition of his Majesty's sloop under my command, and have the honour to be,

" My lord,

" Your lordship's most obedient

" humble servant,

" FRANCIS WM. AUSTEN.

" To the Rt. Hon. Lord Nelson, K.B.,

Etc., etc., etc."

" *May* 14.—At four o'clock hove to in Palermo Bay. The first lieutenant returned on board. At six o'clock filled and made all sail on the larboard tack, pinnace ahead towing."

Nelson was at this time short of small vessels by which to send news. He therefore employed the *Peterel* to go on to the blockading squadron off Malta with orders, which were delivered on board H.M.S. *Goliath*, about noon on May 19. The *Peterel* then returned to Minorca.

Bruix, contrary to expectation, did nothing with his chance. Probably the aim of the Directory in sending him was to discover how far Spain was to be relied upon for support, and there may have been no intention of employing

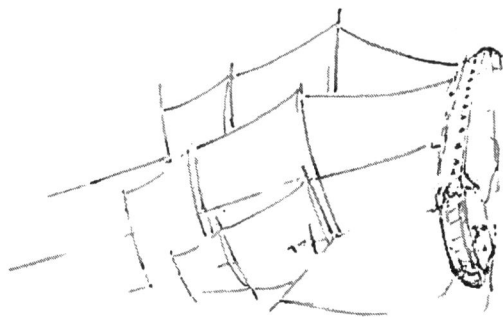

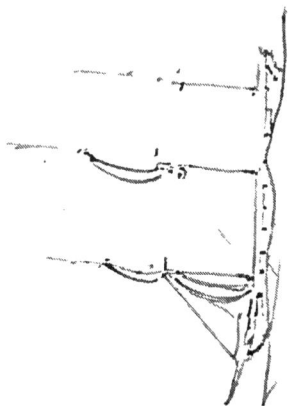

SLOOP OF WAR AND FRIGATE

The *Peterel* Sloop

him to help Bonaparte, but Bruix seems to
have had a free hand in the matter, so that his
own want of resolution and failure of insight are
the apparent causes of the expedition proving
inconclusive.

The Spanish fleet came out of Cadiz, as was
of course to be expected, and on May 30
Bruix sailed eastward from Toulon, getting into
communication with General Moreau at Genoa.
The great matter was to keep the two fleets
from combining, and this might be done by
following the French fleet and beating it. Lord
St. Vincent's health now entirely gave way, and
he was obliged to give up the command to Keith,
though it is probable he expected to have his
advice still followed. Lord Keith sailed away in
pursuit, but Bruix doubled on his tracks, and
keeping close in shore repassed Toulon, and got
down to Cartagena, where he met the Spanish
fleet. Keith, instead of taking up the commanding position earnestly recommended by St. Vincent, let his chance slip by going back to Minorca,
which he supposed to be in danger, and thus the
conjunction of the fleets took place. It was however followed by no adverse results. Spain was
lukewarm, and Bruix sailed back to Brest, having
accomplished nothing but an addition of fifteen
ships to his fleet, to serve as a pledge for the
goodwill of the Spanish Government. Had Bruix

joined Bonaparte instead of the Spanish fleet, very different results would almost certainly have followed.

The following proclamation will show clearly how important the support of Spain was felt to be, and how anxious Bruix was lest there should be any cause for disagreement.

> " In the name of the French Republic.
> " In the Road of Cartagena, on board the Admiral's sloop the *Ocean*, dated 24th June, in the seventh year of the French Republic, Eustace Bruix commanding the French fleet.

" FRENCHMEN AND REPUBLICANS,—At last, united with our faithful allies, we approach the period when we shall punish England and relieve Europe from all its tyranny. Although I have no doubt, my brave friends, of the sentiments which you have professed, I felt myself bound to call upon you to give proofs of their sincerity by every means in your power. Recollect that it is for the interests of your country, and for your own *honour*, to give to a nation, whom we esteem, the highest opinion of us. That word alone is enough for Frenchmen. Do not above all forget that you are come among a just and generous people, and our most faithful allies. Respect their customs, their usages, their religion. In a

The *Peterel* Sloop

word, let everything be sacred to us. Think the least departure from that which I am now prescribing to you will be a crime in the eyes of the Republic, for which it will be my duty to punish you. But, on the contrary, I am convinced that you will give me an opportunity of praising your conduct, and that will be the greatest recompence I can receive.

"E. BRUIX."

Carrying Lord St. Vincent's letter to Nelson seems to have been the first service of importance which fell to the share of Captain Austen. Perhaps some description of the more ordinary happenings of the life on board of a sloop of war may prove of interest. The change from the position of First Lieutenant on board a ship of the line to that of the Captain of a small vessel must necessarily have been very marked.

Towards the end of 1798 the *Peterel* had had the misfortune to be captured by the Spaniards, who treated the captain (Charles Long) and his crew very badly. The following day she was rescued by the *Argo*, under Captain Bowen. Francis Austen was then given the command, and on February 27 we find him taking over his new duties, the *Peterel* being then moored in Gibraltar Bay.

The first few months were spent in cruising

about the west of the Mediterranean. Almost
every day there was a pursuit of some vessel of
more or less importance. Sometimes "the chace"
proved to be a friendly craft, sometimes she got
away, but not infrequently was captured and
overhauled. On one occasion, Francis Austen
remarks trenchantly, " Our chace proved to be a
tower on the land."

Evidently the plan of procedure was always to
follow up and find out the nationality of any distant sail. If a friend, news was interchanged, and
often some help might be given. If an enemy, an
attack usually followed. One of these small encounters is described in the log of the date March
23, 1799, the *Peterel* then cruising off the south
side of Majorca.

" 11 o'clock.—Saw a latteen-sail boat, appearing
to be a privateer, just within the western point of
Cabrera. From the manœuvres of this boat I judge
her to be a privateer. When we first saw her she
was on the starboard tack, and seemed to be examining us. I could just distinguish her hull from
the Catharpins. She appeared to be full of men.
She was rigged with one large latteen sail, and
might be about fifteen to twenty tons."

This boat was evidently not to be seen again
until " At a quarter past 3, perceived the chace
run round a point of the island into a cove, under
the protection of a castle situated on a high rock.

The *Peterel* Sloop

This was the same boat we saw in the forenoon. Our appearance had evidently frightened them, and they judged it prudent to keep snug till we were gone by, and, at the time they ventured out, supposed us too far off to distinguish them. It was, indeed, with difficulty that we could, as the distance was full three leagues, and their sail was nearly the same colour as the rock along which they were passing.

" The cove or haven into which the boat went is about three-quarters of a mile from the N.W. point of the island, and is completely land-locked by the two points which form it overlapping. We were close in, not more than a quarter of a mile from the westernmost of these points, but could get no ground with forty fathoms line. The castle is situated on a pinnacle rock or cliff on the eastern side of the entrance, and from its situation I should judge it difficult of access to an hostile approach. They had not more than two guns in it, and those were not more than four or six-pounders. Several of their shot went over us, and others fell within a few yards on each side of us, but not one struck the ship. Ours all went on shore, and I believe most of them struck the castle, but there was too much motion to fire with very great precision. This cove, from its situation, is a most excellent place of resort for small privateers, as they are secure from the effects of any wind, and can from

Jane Austen's Sailor Brothers

the height discover the approach of any vessel, and be ready to push out on them when they may be too close to the island to effect their escape."

With nightfall this attack had to be abandoned, and by six o'clock the next morning, March 24, the *Peterel* was in pursuit of another " chace."

"At a quarter past 8, hoisted out the pinnace and launch and sent them to board the chace.

"At 8 o'clock, I could discern with a glass the privateer, with his sail furled, laying in his oars, just within the west point of the cove, ready to pop out on the Spanish boat, and, but for our being so near, certainly would have recaptured her, but when our boats put off from the ship he went in again.

"At 10 o'clock, the boats returned with the chace, which proved to be a Spanish coasting-vessel of 20 tons, from Cadiz bound to Barcelona with wheat, prize to the *General Pigot*, a privateer belonging to Gibraltar. Supplied him with a few baracoes of water.

" At 11 o'clock, in boats and made sail on the larboard tack."

This account of a twenty-four hours on board the *Peterel* will give some idea of the constant interest and continual demand on the judgment incidental to this life. This particular day, though a full one, was barren of results. The privateer got out of the way of the *Peterel*, and the chace

The *Peterel* Sloop

which they did succeed in boarding had already
surrendered to another British ship. The entries
of a few days later, March 28, will show how
varying was the success of these encounters.
On that day they secured three prizes in twelve
hours.

"5 o'clock A.M., saw a strange sail bear S.W.
by S. Bore up and set royal and steering sails
in chace.

"8 o'clock.—Fresh breezes and clear weather ;
came up with the chace close off the west end of
Ivica. Shortened sail and hove to, sent a boat
on board ; she proved to be a Spanish brig laden
with barley, from Almeria bound to Barcelona.
Sent an officer and eight men to take possession,
and took all the Spaniards out of her.

"At 10 o'clock.—Took her in tow, and made
sail to the eastward.

"At half-past 10.—Saw a brig at the south
part of Ivica, cast off the tow, and made all sail
in chace.

"Half-past 11.—In steering sails.

"At noon.—Moderate and clear weather, passing through between Ivica and Formenterra,
prize in company.

"Half-past 12.—Fired five guns at the chace
to make her bring to, but without effect.

"At 1 o'clock.—She anchored close under a
signal tower with four guns on it. Hoisted out

the pinnace, and sent her armed under the direction of the second lieutenant to board the vessel.

"Half-past 2.—The pinnace returned with the brig; sent her away to cut out a small vessel, which was then riding about half a mile to the westward of the tower. The brig appears to be French, but no one was found on board her. Sent an officer and five men to take charge of her.

"At 5 o'clock.—The pinnace returned with the other vessel, a Spanish settee, appearing by papers found on board to be the Alicant packet. Her crew had quitted her on seeing our boats approach. Sent an officer and five men on board to take charge of her. Took her in tow and made sail; prizes in company."

Such days as this were of quite frequent occurrence. Sometimes the prizes were of great value, as on April 11, when the *Peterel*, in company with the *Powerful* and the *Leviathan*, assisted in capturing a vessel which they thought to be a despatch-boat, and therefore of the first importance. She proved to be a fishing-boat, employed in carrying a brigadier-general, a lieutenant-colonel, and a captain of the Walloon Guards over to Ivica from Alicant. She had on board specie to the amount of 9000 dollars. The *Peterel's* share of this valuable prize was 1469

The *Peterel* Sloop

dollars, which was paid out in the following proportions:

To a captain .	.	.	.	.	750	dollars
„ a lieutenant	.	.	.	.	$62\frac{1}{2}$	„
„ a warrant officer	.	.	.	$36\frac{3}{4}$	„
„ a petty officer .	.	.	.	$10\frac{1}{4}$	„
„ a foremast man .	.	.	.	2	„

It is to be feared that the prize-money was a doubtful blessing to the foremast hands, especially as the *Peterel* was then nearing Port Mahon, where they lay at anchor for three days, during which it was no doubt easy to incur the punishments for drunkenness and neglect of duty which we find meted out two days later.

Another capture of political importance is detailed on the 26th April, when a Spanish tartan, the *San Antonio de Padua*, was brought to, having on board fifty-three soldiers belonging to a company of the 3rd battalion of the Walloon Guards, who were being conveyed from Barcelona to Majorca. These, with sailors and a few recruits also on board, summed up a capture of seventy-nine Spanish prisoners, who were taken on board the *Peterel.*

The tartan was manned by a midshipman and seven men, and taken in tow. The prisoners were afterwards transferred to the *Centaur*, and the prize, after everything was taken out of her, was scuttled.

Jane Austen's Sailor Brothers

These few instances will serve to show the kind of life of which we get such tantalising hints in " Persuasion."

The account Captain Wentworth gives to the two Miss Musgroves and to Admiral Croft of his earlier commands is a case in point. The date is not the same, for we remember that Captain Wentworth first got employ in the year six (1806), soon after he had parted in anger from Anne Elliot.

" The Miss Musgroves were just fetching the ' Navy List ' (their own ' Navy List,' the first there had ever been at Uppercross), and sitting down together to pore over it, with the professed view of finding out the ships which Captain Wentworth had commanded.

" ' Your first was the *Asp*, I remember. We will look for the *Asp*.'

" ' You will not find her there. Quite worn out and broken up. I was the last man who commanded her. Hardly fit for service then. Reported fit for home service for a year or two, and so I was sent off to the West Indies.'

" The girls looked all amazement.

" ' The Admiralty,' he continued, ' entertain themselves now and then with sending a few hundred men to sea in a ship not fit to be employed. But they have a great many to provide for ; and among the thousands that may just as well go to

The *Peterel* Sloop

the bottom as not, it is impossible for them to distinguish the very set who may be least missed.'

" ' Phoo! phoo!' cried the Admiral. 'What stuff these young fellows talk! Never was there a better sloop than the *Asp* in her day. For an old built sloop you would not see her equal. Lucky fellow to get her! He knows there must have been twenty better men than himself applying for her at the same time. Lucky fellow to get anything so soon, with no more interest than his.'

" ' I felt my luck, Admiral, I assure you,' replied Captain Wentworth seriously. 'I was as well satisfied with my appointment as you can desire. It was a great object with me at the time to be at sea; a very great object. I wanted to be doing something.'

" ' To be sure you did. What should a young fellow like you do ashore for half a year together? If a man has not a wife, he soon wants to be afloat again.'

" ' But, Captain Wentworth,' cried Louisa, ' how vexed you must have been when you came to the *Asp*, to see what an old thing they had given you.'

" ' I knew pretty well what she was before that day,' said he smiling. 'I had no more discoveries to make than you would have as to the fashion

and strength of an old pelisse, which you had seen
lent about among half your acquaintance ever
since you could remember, and which at last on
some very wet day is lent to yourself. Ah! she
was a dear old *Asp* to me. She did all I wanted.
I knew she would. I knew that we should either
go to the bottom together, or that she would be the
making of me ; and I never had two days of foul
weather all the time I was at sea in her ; and after
taking privateers enough to be very entertaining, I
had the good luck in my passage home the next
autumn to fall in with the very French frigate I
wanted. I brought her into Plymouth ; and here
was another instance of luck. We had not been
six hours in the Sound when a gale came on
which lasted four days and four nights, and which
would have done for poor old *Asp* in half the
time, our touch with the Great Nation not having
improved our condition. Four and twenty hours
later and I should only have been a gallant Captain Wentworth in a small paragraph at one
corner of the newspapers ; and being lost in only
a sloop, nobody would have thought about me.'

"The girls were now hunting for the *Laconia ;*
and Captain Wentworth could not deny himself
the pleasure of taking the precious volume into
his own hands to save them the trouble, and once
more read aloud the little statement of her name
and rate, and present non-commissioned class·

The *Peterel* Sloop

Observing over it that she too had been one of the best friends man ever had.

"'Ah, those were pleasant days when I had the *Laconia*! How fast I made money in her! A friend of mine and I had such a lovely cruise together off the Western Islands. Poor Harville, sister! You know how much he wanted money : worse than myself. He had a wife. Excellent fellow! I shall never forget his happiness. He felt it all so much for her sake. I wished for him again next summer, when I had still had the same luck in the Mediterranean.'"

One cannot but feel, when one comes on such a conversation in Jane Austen's novel, how perfectly she understood the details of her brothers' lives. Her interest and sympathy were so great that we can almost hear Francis and Charles recounting experiences to their home circle, with a delicious dwelling on the dangers, for the sake of inward shudders, or "more open exclamations of pity and horror" from their hearers, with sidelong hits at the Admiralty, and with the true sailor's love of, and pride in, the vessels he has commanded.

CHAPTER VI

THE PATROL OF THE MEDITERRANEAN

IT will be remembered that at the close of 1796
scarcely a British man-of-war was to be seen in
the Mediterranean. To estimate the work that
St. Vincent and Nelson had since accomplished,
it is only necessary to say that by the summer of
1799 the British Navy was everywhere, blockading
Genoa and Malta, patrolling the Egyptian and
Syrian coasts, and in possession of Minorca,
while Nelson was stationed at Palermo. The
French armies in Italy were cut off from reinforcements by our ships before Genoa. Bonaparte's soldiers in Egypt were equally helpless,
though he himself managed to get home in spite
of the danger of capture.

Attempts were of course made by the French
to change this position. Rear-Admiral Perrée
had served on the immense fleet which Bonaparte
took to Egypt in 1798, and there was appointed
to the command of the light flotilla intended to
patrol the Nile. Most of his seniors were shortly

The Patrol of the Mediterranean

afterwards killed or captured by Nelson's fleet in Aboukir Bay, and he then took charge of the remaining frigates which had safely anchored at Alexandria, and which were compelled to remain there, as Captain Troubridge had established a blockade of the coast. When Bonaparte marched for Syria, early in 1799, Perrée was ordered to bring battering cannon to Haifa for the attack on Acre. It was some time before he got the opportunity to slip out of Alexandria, and he then found Jaffa the only place available for landing the guns. Accomplishing this, he vainly endeavoured to co-operate in the siege of Acre, but was driven off by the *Tigre* and *Theseus* under Sir Sydney Smith. The blockade made it impossible for Perrée to re-enter Alexandria. The five vessels therefore sailed for Toulon, and on June 18 we have in the log of the *Peterel* the account of the capture of this unlucky squadron, within a few hours of their French haven.

June 17.—"Admiral (Lord Keith) and fleet in company. The *Emerald* made signal for five sail in sight. The Admiral signalled for general chace. Answered his signal to us to keep between the Admiral and the chacing ships in N.E., to repeat signals. At 8 P.M. *Emerald* N.E., six or seven miles, Admiral west, four miles.

June 18.—"One o'clock P.M. Saw four sail bearing N.W. At six, five sail of strangers in sight.

Jane Austen's Sailor Brothers

At seven, perceived the *Centaur* open a fire on the chace, which was returned. Saw two of them strike and shorten sail. Half-past seven, the *Emerald* got up with, and took possession of, another. At eight o'clock the *Centaur* brought to a fourth. The *Success* and the *Triton* in chace of the fifth.

June 19.—"At daylight, ten of the fleet and five prizes in company. Boats of the fleet employed on the 19th getting the prisoners out of the prizes. These ships proved to be a squadron which had escaped out of Alexandria on the 19th of March, and, after cruising a considerable time off Joppa, were returning to Toulon. Their names are as follows :

La Junon .	.	38 guns, 600 men (with a Rear-Admiral on board).
L'Alceste .	.	36 guns.
La Courageuse .		32 guns, 300 men.
L'Alerte .	.	16-gun brig.
La Salamine	.	16-gun ditto."

Marshal Suwarrow, in command of the Russian and Austrian armies, was now making use of Bonaparte's enforced detention in Egypt to drive the French out of Italy. By June, after the battle of the Trebbia, he had not only shut up Moreau's army in Genoa, but had driven Macdonald back into Tuscany. It was only with the greatest difficulty that the two French

The Patrol of the Mediterranean

commanders were able eventually to join forces in Genoa. With characteristic want of confidence in their generals, the French Directory sent out General Joubert to take command in the place of the two who had been worsted. Almost immediately after his arrival, he was himself utterly defeated and killed at the battle of Novi. Nothing was left of the French possessions in Italy except Genoa, and a few smaller fortified places. To Genoa Massena came after his successful exploits in Switzerland, and made his memorable stand, against the Austrian army besieging by land and the British blockading by sea.

With these events during 1799 and 1800, the *Peterel* was in constant touch. On one occasion, off Savona, a vessel was taken containing two hundred and fifty wounded soldiers, who were being conveyed from Genoa back to France after the indecisive battle of the Trebbia. On this Captain Austen remarks, "As many of them were in such a state as not to be moved but at the risque of their lives, Captain Caulfield (of the *Aurora*), from motives of humanity, let the vessel proceed."

Another capture shows how much the French were hampered by our blockade, their general being unable to reach his army excepting by sea. In Francis Austen's own words :

Jane Austen's Sailor Brothers

August 2, 1799.—" Last night at 9 P.M. the *Minerve's* boats came alongside ; sent them along with our own, armed, under the command of the first lieutenant to cut out some vessels from the Bay of Diano.

" About midnight saw a very heavy fire of cannon and musketry in Diano Bay. Towards dawn the boats returned on board, having brought out a large settee laden with wine, and a French armed half-galley, mounting six guns, and rowing twenty-six oars. This galley had lately arrived from Toulon with General Joubert, appointed to supersede Moreau in the command of the French army of Italy, and was to have proceeded to-day with the general to the headquarters, near Genoa. She was manned with thirty-six people, twenty of which jumped overboard and swam ashore as soon as our boats attacked them. The other sixteen were made prisoners, amongst which was the commander of her, having the rank of ensign de vaisseau in the service of the Republic. The vessel is called *La Virginie*, is Turkish built, and was taken by the French at Malta when they got possession of that place last year."

Another time the chace is described as follows :

July 14.—" This vessel proved to be the *El Fortunato* Spanish ship polacre of about 100 tons burden, from Cagliari bound to Oneglia, laden with wine, and having on board an officer

The Patrol of the Mediterranean

charged with despatches from the King of Sardinia to General Suwarrow, Commander-in-Chief of the combined armies of Russia and Austria in Italy."

The autumn and winter of 1799 were spent by the *Peterel* cruising again in the west of the Mediterranean, chiefly off Minorca; but in the spring of 1800 they were again near Marseilles. The capture of the French brig *La Ligurienne*, described in the following letter, is another witness to the fruitless attempts of the French to get help to the army which Bonaparte had left behind in Egypt.

"Peterel AT SEA, *March* 22, 1800.

"SIR,—I have to inform you that the vessels with which you saw me engaged yesterday afternoon near Cape Couronne, were a ship, brig, and xebecque, belonging to the French Republic; two of which, the ship and xebecque, I drove on shore, and, after a running action of about one hour and a half, during the most of which we were not more than two cables length from the shore, and frequently not half that distance, the third struck her colours. On taking possession, we found her to be *La Ligurienne*, French national brig, mounting fourteen six-pounders, and two thirty-six-pound howitzers, all brass, commanded by François Auguste Pelabon, lieutenant de vaisseau, and had on board at the commencement of the action

83

one hundred and four men. Though from the spirited conduct and alacrity of Lieutenant Packer, Mr. Thompson, the master, and Mr. Hill, the purser (who very handsomely volunteered his services at the main deck guns), joined to the gallantry and determined courage of the rest of the officers, seamen and marines of his Majesty's sloop under my command, I was happily enabled to bring the contest to a favourable issue; yet I could not but feel the want, and regret the absence, of my first lieutenant, Mr. Glover, and thirty men, who were at the time away in prizes. I have a lively pleasure in that this service has been performed without a man hurt on our part, and with no other damage to the ship than four of our carronades dismounted, and a few shots through the sails. *La Ligurienne* is a very fine vessel of the kind, well equipped with stores of all sorts, in excellent repair, and not two years old. She is built on a peculiar plan, being fastened throughout with screw bolts, so as to be taken to pieces and put together with ease, and is said to have been intended to follow Bonaparte to Egypt. I learn from the prisoners that the ship is called *Le Cerf*, mounting fourteen six-pounders, xebecque *Le Joillet*, mounting six six-pounders, and that they had sailed in company with a convoy (two of which, as per margin, I captured in the forenoon) that morning from Cette, bound to Marseilles. I

PETEREL IN ACTION WITH *LA LIGURIENNE* NEAR MARSEILLES, MARCH 21, 1800

The Patrol of the Mediterranean

enclose a return of the killed and wounded, as far as I have been able to ascertain it,

"And am, your very humble servant,
"FRANCIS WM. AUSTEN.

"To Robert Dudley Oliver, Esq.,
"Captain of H.M. Ship *Mermaid*.

"Return of killed and wounded in an action between his Britannic Majesty's sloop *Peterel*, Francis Wm. Austen, Esq., Commander, and the French national brig *La Ligurienne*, commanded by François Auguste Pelabon, lieutenant de vaisseau.

"*Peterel:* Killed, none; wounded, none.

"*La Ligurienne:* Killed, the captain and one seaman; wounded, one gardemarin and one seaman.
"(Signed)   FRANCIS WM. AUSTEN."

The captures, "as per margin," are of a French bark, name unknown, about two hundred and fifty tons, and of a French bombarde, *La Vestic*, about one hundred and fifty tons, both laden with wheat, and both abandoned by their crews on the *Peterel's* attack.

If, as is stated, *La Ligurienne* was intended to go to Egypt, it seems not improbable that the reason for her peculiar construction was that she might be taken to pieces, carried across the desert, and launched again in the Red Sea, there to take part in an attempt on India.

This exploit, though related in a matter-of-fact way by Captain Austen in his letter, was not inconsiderable in the eyes of the authorities, and the result was his immediate promotion to post rank. He himself knew nothing of this advancement until the following October; only an instance of the slowness and difficulty of communication, which was so great a factor in the naval affairs of that time.

It should be mentioned that the frigate *Mermaid* was in sight during part of this action, which perhaps had something to do with the two French vessels running themselves ashore, also that the capture of *La Ligurienne* was within six miles of Marseilles. The *Peterel* took her three prizes to Minorca, where the prisoners were sent on board the *Courageuse*, one of Perrée's frigates captured in 1799 as already described.

The next voyage was to Malta, where the fortress of Valetta was still in French hands, with a few ships under the command of Rear-Admiral Villeneuve. The British blockading squadron had just taken the *Guillaume Tell* in the endeavour to escape from Valetta harbour, after eighteen months' stay. This ship of the line was the only one remaining to the French from Bonaparte's expedition to Egypt and the Battle of the Nile.

The Patrol of the Mediterranean

The *Peterel* took on board, in the Bay of Marsa
Sirocco, thirty-five of the crew of the *Guillaume
Tell*, by orders of Commodore Troubridge of the
Culloden, and with these prisoners made sail for
Palermo, where for a few days she hoisted Nelson's
flag. Arrived once more at Port Mahon, in
Minorca, the French sailors were added to the
number on the *Courageuse*, and the *Peterel* found
her way to Lord Keith's fleet, now closely invest-
ing General Massena in Genoa.

The great events of the campaign of Marengo
are matters of European history. The British
fleet's blockade of the coast was clearly a deter-
mining factor in the choice of the St. Bernard
route by the First Consul, inasmuch as the
Riviera road was commanded from the sea. It
must remain a question whether Bonaparte deli-
berately left Massena's army to risks of starvation
and capture, in order that the destruction of the
Austrian forces in Piedmont might be complete.
Massena had been compelled to extend his lines
too far, so that he might secure from a moun-
tainous country the supplies which could not
reach him from France. This made it possible
for the Austrians to press their advantage, and to
isolate the fortresses of Nice, Savona, and Genoa.
The unceasing patrol of the sea completed the
circle of hostile forces. The French army was
entirely shut up in Genoa, and throughout the

month of May the town was several times bombarded by the ships and the armed boats of the fleet. These armed boats had already reduced the small garrison of Savona. It is recorded in the *Peterel* log that a "polacre laden with artillery and ammunition for the army of General Baron d'Ott" came from that port. The *Peterel* was detailed by Lord Keith to cruise in shore as near as possible to Genoa, and Captain Austen received the thanks of this Admiral for his energetic performance of that duty. One night the vessel was under fire from the lighthouse forts, and received several shots. A feature of the blockade was the plan of "rowing guard" each night, in order to prevent access to the harbour after dark. The *Peterel's* pinnace was frequently on this duty in turn with the other boats of the fleet, and took part in cutting out the *Prima* galley after midnight on the 21st of May. This galley was intended to take part in an attempt on the smaller vessels of the British fleet, but was attacked by the boats' crews at the Mole when just ready to come out. She was boarded in the most gallant manner, in spite of a large force of fighting men on board, and of a heavy fire from the harbour forts. The capture was greatly helped by the conduct of the 300 galley slaves, who rowed out so fast that they almost outstripped the boats that were towing her. These slaves were allowed on

The Patrol of the Mediterranean

deck when the prize was out of gunshot range from the harbour, and great were their manifestations of joy at their release. The sequel of the incident was tragic. Lord Keith sent most of them back to Genoa with the other French prisoners, no doubt with the idea of forcing their support on the half-starved garrison. The galley slaves were shot as traitors in the market-place.

During the preliminary conference with General d'Ott and Lord Keith, preceding the French surrender at Genoa, it is said that some contempt for Austria was expressed by Massena, who went on as follows : " Milord, si jamais la France et l'Angleterre s'entendre, elles gouverneraient la monde." This almost foreshadows the " entente cordiale " of 1904.

On June 4 the French army capitulated. Genoa town was handed over to the Austrians under General Melas, and the port was occupied by Lord Keith in his flagship *Minotaur*.

But already the First Consul had descended into Italy, had taken possession of Milan, and was in full march to defeat Baron d'Ott at Montebello. On the 14th Marengo was fought, and the tide of fortune turned. Genoa, Savona, and all the fortresses of Piedmont were made over to the French. Massena came back on June 24, and Lord Keith had just time to move out of the harbour and to resume his

Jane Austen's Sailor Brothers

blockade. The victorious First Consul was again in full possession of Northern Italy.

Before the end of May the *Peterel* was already on her way southward, and the log records the transport of thirty-two men to H.M.S. *Guillaume Tell* (recently captured) off Syracuse, then another call at Malta (St. Paul's Bay) where the blockaders were busy with the later stages of the reduction of Valetta. The destination of the *Peterel* was the coast of Egypt, where Sir Sydney Smith was locally in command. Alexandria and other harbours were still held by the French, now quite cut off from outside support. A Turkish fleet of twelve ships was at anchor off Alexandria, and the blockade was supposed to be maintained by them, but in actual practice the burden devolved upon the three British vessels, *Tigre*, *Transfer*, and *Peterel*. They appear to have joined forces at Jaffa, and to have cruised off the Egyptian coast, with an occasional visit to Cyprus, for some months. They were all this time without news from England.

The allied fleets of France and Spain were by no means inactive, and, though they did not accomplish much in the Mediterranean, there was always a serious risk for a single vessel, and despatch-boats were particularly unsafe carrying, as they did, intelligence that might be useful to the enemy. At this time the Spanish ports in

The Patrol of the Mediterranean

the neighbourhood of Gibraltar were strongly
held, and it was a great object with the British
Government to relieve this pressure, which seriously threatened their communications with the
whole of the Mediterranean. Algeciras was specially dangerous, and we find constant attacks upon
the enemy there, in which Charles Austen as
Lieutenant of the *Endymion* had a considerable
part, under Sir Thomas Williams and his successor
Captain Philip Durham. His service was varied
by the capture of several privateers, among others
of *La Furie*. The *Endymion* afterwards convoyed
ten Indiamen home from St. Helena, for which
service Captain Durham received the thanks of
the East India Company. On the occasion of
the capture of the *Scipio*, Lieutenant Charles
Austen specially distinguished himself. The encounter took place in a violent gale, but, in spite
of wind and weather, he put off in a boat with
only four men, and boarded the vessel, which had
just surrendered. The *Scipio* was a fine craft of
18 guns, manned by 140 men.

Charles was particularly lucky at this time in
his shares of prize-money. Jane tells us in one
of her letters to Cassandra how generously he
spent it.

"Charles has received £30 for his share of the
privateer, and expects £10 more ; but of what
avail is it to take prizes if he lays out the produce

in presents for his sisters?   He has been buying
gold chains and topaz crosses for us.   He must be
well scolded.   I shall write again by this post to
thank and reproach him.   We shall be unbearably
fine."

It is a good instance of the way in which Jane
Austen " worked up " her incidents that the
brother's present of a cross and a gold chain
should form the groundwork on which is built up
the story of Fanny's flutterings of heart over her
adornments for the ball at Mansfield.

"The 'how she should be dressed' was a point
of painful solicitude; and the almost solitary orna-
ment in her possession, a very pretty amber cross
which William had brought her from Sicily, was
the greatest distress of all, for she had nothing
but a bit of riband to fasten it to; and though
she had worn it in that manner once, would it be
allowable at such a time, in the midst of all the
rich ornaments which she supposed all the other
young ladies would appear in?   And yet not to
wear it!   William had wanted to buy her a gold
chain too, but the purchase had been beyond his
means, and therefore not to wear the cross might
be mortifying to him.   These were anxious con-
siderations; enough to sober her spirits even
under the prospect of a ball given principally for
her gratitfication."

Then follows Miss Crawford's gift of a necklace

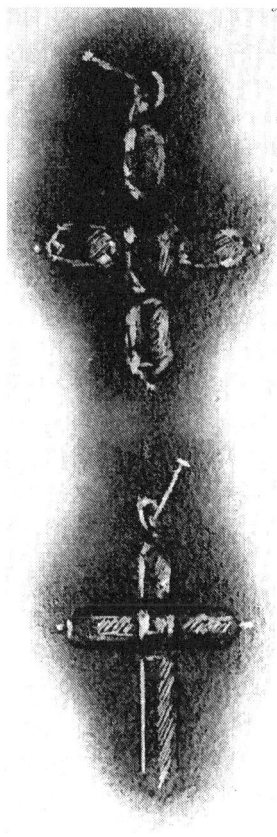

THE TOPAZ CROSSES GIVEN TO
CASSANDRA AND JANE BY
CHARLES AUSTEN

The Patrol of the Mediterranean

to wear with the cross, with all its alarming associations with Henry Crawford ; then Edmund's gift of a chain ; her resolve to wear Miss Crawford's gift to please him ; and lastly the delightful discovery that the necklace was too large for the purpose. Edmund's chain, "therefore, must be worn ; and having, with delightful feelings, joined the chain and the cross, those memorials of the two most beloved of her heart ; those dearest tokens so formed for each other by everything real and imaginary, and put them round her neck, and seen and felt how full of William and Edmund they were, she was able, without an effort, to resolve on wearing Miss Crawford's necklace too. She acknowledged it to be right. Miss Crawford had a claim ; and when it was no longer to encroach on, to interfere with the stronger claims, the truer kindness of another, she could do her justice even with pleasure to herself. The necklace really looked very well ; and Fanny left her room at last, comfortably satisfied with herself and all about her."

CHAPTER VII

AT HOME AND ABROAD

The truism that absence strengthens more ties than it weakens is clearly demonstrated by the letters of the Austen family. In spite of the difficulty of sending letters, and the doubt of their reaching England, the brothers managed to get news through whenever it was possible. To know that their efforts were appreciated one has only to read how every scrap of this news was sent from one sister to the other in the constant letters they interchanged on those rare occasions when they were parted. The Austen family had always a certain reserve in showing affection, but the feeling which appears in this longing for tidings, in the gentle satires on small failings or transient love-affairs of their brothers, combined with the occasional "dear Frank" or "dear Charles," was one which stood the test of time, and was transmitted to the brothers' children in a way that made the names of "Aunt Jane" and "Aunt Cassandra" stand for all that was

At Home and Abroad

lovable in the thoughts of their nephews and nieces.

The scarcity of letters must have been a severe trial. Just at this time, when those at home knew of Frank's promotion, and he had as yet no idea of it, the longing to send and receive news must have been very great. He was hard at work in the summer of 1800 with Sir Sydney Smith's squadron off Alexandria. From there, early in July, he wrote to Cassandra. This letter was received at Steventon on November 1, when Cassandra was at Godmersham with Edward, so Jane sent her word of its arrival. "We have at last heard from Frank; a letter from him to you came yesterday, and I mean to send it on as soon as I can get a ditto (that means a frank), which I hope to do in a day or two. *En attendant*, you must rest satisfied with knowing that on the 8th of July the *Peterel* with the rest of the Egyptian squadron was off the Isle of Cyprus, whither they went from Jaffa for provisions, &c., and whence they were to sail in a day or two for Alexandria, there to await the English proposals for the eva- cuation of Egypt. The rest of the letter, accord- ing to the present fashionable style of composi- tion, is chiefly descriptive. Of his promotion he knows nothing; of prizes he is guiltless."

An event which would no doubt have made a point of interest in this letter happened the day

after it was sent, but is recorded in the log for
July 9:

" Received two oxen and fifty-two gallons of
wine, being the *Peterel's* portion of a present from
the Governor of the Island."

The same letter from Jane to her sister contains news of Charles, who had been at home
comparatively lately, and was on the *Endymion*,
which was "waiting only for orders, but may wait
for them perhaps a month." Three weeks later
he was at home again.

" Naughty Charles did not come on Tuesday,
but good Charles came yesterday morning. About
two o'clock he walked in on a Gosport hack. His
feeling equal to such a fatigue is a good sign, and
his feeling no fatigue a still better. He walked
down to Deane to dinner, he danced the whole
evening, and to-day is no more tired than a gentleman ought to be. Your desiring to hear from me
on Sunday will, perhaps, bring you a more particular account of the ball than you may care for,
because one is prone to think more of such things
the morning after they happen, than when time
has entirely driven them out of one's recollection.

" It was a pleasant evening; Charles found it
remarkably so, but I cannot tell why, unless the
absence of Miss Terry, towards whom his con-
science reproaches him with being now perfectly
indifferent, was a relief to him.

At Home and Abroad

"Summers has made my gown very well indeed, and I get more and more pleased with it. Charles does not like it, but my father and Mary do. My mother is very much resigned to it, and as for James he gives it the preference over everything of the kind he ever saw, in proof of which I am desired to say that if you like to sell yours Mary will buy it.

"Farewell! Charles sends *you* his best love, and Edward his worst. If you think the distinction improper, you may take the worst yourself. He will write to you when he gets back to his ship, and in the meantime desires that you will consider me as your affectionate sister J. A.

"P.S. Charles is in very good looks indeed. . . .

"I rejoice to say that we have just had another letter from our dear Frank. It is to you, very short, written from Larnaca in Cyprus, and so lately as October 2nd. He came from Alexandria, and was to return there in three or four days, knew nothing of his promotion, and does not write above twenty lines, from a doubt of the letter's ever reaching you, and an idea of all letters being opened at Vienna. He wrote a few days before to you from Alexandria by the *Mercury*, sent with despatches to Lord Keith. Another letter must be owing to us besides this, *one* if not *two;* because none of these are for me."

The scenes of home life which these extracts

give us form a strong contrast to the readings in the log of the *Peterel* between the dates of Frank's two letters.

In spite of the fact that viewed as a whole this was a breathing space between engagements, each side standing back to recover and to watch for the next movement on the part of the other, yet, in detail, it was a time of activity.

Now and then, in the log, occurs the chace of a germe (or djerm) carrying supplies for the French, and a boat expedition is organised to cut out one or two of these craft, from an inlet where they had taken refuge.

"At twelve the boats returned without the germe, having perceived her to be under the protection of a field piece and a body of soldiers." Next day one was captured "with only 17 bales of tobacco on board" (Captain Austen was not a smoker). Then " condemned by survey the remaining part of the best bower cable as unserviceable." " Held a survey on and condemned a cask of rice." " The senior lieutenant was surveyed by the surgeons of the squadron and found to be a fit object for invaliding."

The next incident is described in the following report :

"*Peterel*, OFF ALEXANDRIA, *August* 14, 1800.

" SIR,—On the morning of the 10th, the day subsequent to my parting with the *Tigre*, I joined

At Home and Abroad

the Turkish squadron off this place, consisting of one ship of the line, and three corvettes under the command of Injee Bey, captain of the gallies, with whom I concerted on the most proper distribution of the force left with him. It was finally agreed that one corvette should be stationed off Aboukir, a second off Alexandria, and the third off the Tower of Marabout, the line-of-battle ship and the *Peterel* occasionally to visit the different points of the station as we might judge fit. It blowing too hard to admit of any germes passing, I thought it advisable to stretch to the westward as far as the Arab's Tower, off which I continued till the afternoon of the 12th, when I stood back to the eastward, and was somewhat surprised to see none of the Turkish squadron off Alexandria. At 8 o'clock the following morning, having an offing of three or four leagues, I stood in for the land, and in about an hour saw three of the Turkish ships a long way to the Eastward, and the fourth, which proved to be the line-of-battle ship, laying totally dismasted, on the Reef, about halfway between the Castle and Island of Aboukir. Thinking it possible, from what little I knew of Aboukir Bay, to get the *Peterel* within gunshot of her, and by that means to disperse the swarm of germes which surrounded her, and whose crews I could plainly discern busy in plundering, I stood in round the east side of the island, and anchored in quarter less four fathoms, a long gun-shot distance from her, and sent Mr. Thompson, the master, in the pinnace to sound in a direction towards her, in order to ascertain whether it was practicable to get any nearer with the ship, and if he met with no resistance (the germes having all made sail before we anchored) to board and set fire to the wreck. Though it blew very strong, and the boat had to row nearly two miles, almost directly to windward, yet by the great exertions of the officers and boat's crew, in an hour and twenty minutes I had the satisfaction of seeing the wreck in a perfect blaze, and the boat returning. Mr. Thompson brought back with him thirteen Greek sailors, part of the crew, and one Arab left in their hurry by the germes.

"From the Greeks I collected that the ship went on shore while in the act of wearing about 9 o'clock on the night of the 11th, that about half the crew had been taken on board the corvettes, and the Bey, with the principal part of the officers and the rest of the crew, having surrendered to the French, had landed the next evening at Aboukir. At the time we stood in, the French had 300 men at work on board the wreck, endeavouring to save the guns, but had only succeeded in landing one from the quarter-deck.

"Shortly after my anchoring I sent an officer to the corvette, which had followed us in, and an-

At Home and Abroad

chored near to us, to inform their commander what I proposed doing, and to desire the assistance of their boats in case of resistance from any persons who might be remaining on board the wreck, a demand which they did not think proper to comply with, alleging that, as all the cloathes, &c., had been landed, there was nothing of value remaining, and besides that it would be impossible to get on board, as the French had a guard of soldiers in her.

" I cannot sufficiently praise the zeal and activity with which Mr. Thompson and the nine men with him performed this service, by which I trust the greatest part, if not all, of the guns, and other useful parts of the wreck, have been prevented from falling into the hands of the enemy. The thirteen Greeks I sent on board one of the Turkish corvettes, and intend, as soon as I have communication with the shore, to land the Arab.

" I have the honour to be, Sir,
" Your obedient servant,
" FRANCIS WM. AUSTEN.

" To Sir Sydney Smith, K.S.,
" Senior officer of H.M. Ships and Vessels
"employed in the Levant."

The French were quite ready to take possession of all that the predatory Arab germes were likely to leave on board the Turkish line-of-battle ship.

Jane Austen's Sailor Brothers

There was of course much less difficulty in getting the *Peterel* into Aboukir Bay than in navigating the larger corvettes of the Turks; but, where Nelson had brought in his fleet, before the Battle of the Nile, there was water enough for any vessel, if properly handled.

The following letters give the conclusion of the matter:

"His Britannic Majesty's Sloop *Peterel*, off Alexandria,
"*August* 16, 1800.

"Sir,—I avail myself of the present flag to set on shore with an unconditional release eleven Arabs, prisoners of war. Should it be not inconsistent with the instructions you may be acting under, the release of an equal number of the subjects of the Sublime Porte will be considered as a fair return.

"I have the honour to be, &c.,
"Your obedient servant,
"F. W. Austen.
"To General Lanusse,
"Commandant of Alexandria."

"*Peterel*, off Alexandria, *August* 7.

"Sir,—The *King George* transport is this morning arrived here from Rhodes, and as I find, by the report of the master, that the object of his mission in landing the powder has not been accomplished, I shall send him off directly with orders to

At Home and Abroad

follow you agreeable to given rendezvous. . . . I enclose herewith a letter received five days ago by a Turkish transport from Jaffa; one from myself containing the particulars of the loss of the Turkish line-of-battle ship, a copy of my letter to General Lanusse, which accompanied the Arabs on shore yesterday (the first day since my leaving the *Tigre*, that the weather has been sufficiently moderate to admit of communicating with the shore), and lastly a letter from the Vizir, which I received yesterday from Jaffa by a Turkish felucca. As the weather becomes more settled I hope to annoy the germes, though I must not count on any support or assistance from the Turks, as Injee Bey, when I first joined him, declared he had received directions from the Capitan Pacha not to molest them. Two of the corvettes are gone to join the Capitan Pacha, but this I learnt only two days after they went. The officer who accompanied the flag yesterday could not obtain any certain intelligence of Captain Boyle and his people, for in answer to his inquiries he was told they were still at or near Cairo.

"I have the honour to be, &c.

"To Sir Wm. Sydney Smith, K.S.,
  "Senior officer of H.M. Ships and Vessels
    "employed in the Levant."

This Capitan Pacha was a man of some note.

Jane Austen's Sailor Brothers

His career is an example of the inefficacy of the greatest talents under such a government as that of Turkey. He was in every way an able man—strong and determined—considering all circumstances not to be called cruel—enlightened in his ideas. His chief lack was that of education, but he was anxious to learn from all. He had great respect for Europeans and sympathy with their outlook. Altogether, though he did a great work for the Turkish navy—improving the construction of the ships—taking care that the officers should be properly educated, and drawing the supply of men from the best possible sources, and all this in a country where reform seemed a hopeless task, yet, so great was the power of his personality, that one is more surprised that he did so little than that he did so much.

The Captain Courtney Boyle spoken of in this letter was evidently an acquaintance of the family, as we find him mentioned in one of Jane's letters. His ship, the *Cormorant*, had been wrecked on the Egyptian coast, and the whole crew made prisoners by the French. He must have obtained his release very shortly afterwards, for the following letter from Jane to Cassandra was clearly written when the family at Steventon were looking forward to Frank's return, but before they had direct news from himself:

" I should not have thought it necessary to write

At Home and Abroad

to you so soon, but for the arrival of a letter from Charles to myself. It was written last Saturday from off the Start, and conveyed to Popham Lane by Captain Boyle, on his way to Midgham. He came from Lisbon in the *Endymion*. I will copy Charles's account of his conjectures about Frank : ' He has not seen my brother lately, nor does he expect to find him arrived, as he met Captain Inglis at Rhodes, going up to take command of the *Peterel* as he was coming down ; but supposes he will arrive in less than a fortnight from this time, in some ship which is expected to reach England about that time with despatches from Sir Ralph Abercrombie.' The event must show what sort of a conjurer Captain Boyle is. The *Endymion* has not been plagued with any more prizes. Charles spent three pleasant days in Lisbon. When this letter was written, the *Endymion* was becalmed, but Charles hoped to reach Portsmouth by Monday or Tuesday. He received my letter, communicating our plans, before he left England ; was much surprised, of course, but is quite reconciled to them, and means to come to Steventon once more while Steventon is ours."

Captain Charles Inglis, who was to succeed Francis Austen, had served as lieutenant in the *Penelope*, and specially distinguished himself in the capture of the *Guillaume Tell*.

While these conjectures as to Frank's whereabouts and the possible date of his return were passing between his relations at home, he had been still pursuing the ordinary round of duties such as are described in this letter, quite ignorant until the actual event of any approaching change either for them or for himself.

"SIR,—I have to inform you that I anchored with his Majesty's sloop under my command at Larnaca on the evening of the 1st instant, where I completed my water, and purchased as much wine as the ship would stow, but was not able to procure any bread, as from the great exports of corn which have been lately made to supply the Vizir's army in Syria, the inhabitants are almost in a state of famine. I sailed from Larnaca the evening of the 6th, and anchored here on the 9th at noon. As I had only five days' bread on board I have judged it proper to take on board 50 quintals of that which had been prepared for the *Tigre*, and not being acquainted with the price agreed on, have directed the purser to leave a certificate with the Dragoman of the Porte, for the quantity received, that it may be included with the *Tigre's* vouchers, and settled for with the purser of that ship.

"The Governor of Nicosia made application to me yesterday in the name of the Capitan Pacha for assistance to enable him to get a gun on shore

At Home and Abroad

from one of the gun-boats which has been wrecked here, which, tho' I knew would detain me a day, I thought it right to comply with ; the gun has been to-day got on shore, and I am now going to weigh. I propose stretching more towards Alexandria if the wind is not very unfavourable, and should I find no counter orders, shall afterwards put in execution the latter part of yours of the 23rd ult.

"I have directed the captain of the *Kirling Gech*, which I found here on my arrival without orders, to wait till the 16th for the arrival of the *Tigre*, when, if not otherwise directed, to proceed to Rhodes, and follow such orders or information as he may obtain there.

"I have the honor to be, &c.,

"To Sir Sydney Smith."

"The latter part of yours of the 23rd " possibly refers to instructions to proceed to Rhodes, for we find in the log that the *Peterel* went on there early in October, and there at last Captain Austen was greeted with the news of his promotion to Post Rank. The *Peterel* anchored in the Road of Rhodes at ten o'clock on the morning of October 20, where the *Tigre* was 21 days at anchor, and at this point the private log of the *Peterel* stops short.

Although we have no account from Francis

Jane Austen's Sailor Brothers

Austen himself of his meeting with Captain Inglis, he evidently wrote a lively description of the incident to his sisters. Jane writes from Steventon on January 21st to Cassandra: "Well, and so Frank's letter has made you very happy, but you are afraid he would not have patience to stay for the *Haarlem*, which you wish him to have done, as being safer than the merchantman." Frank's great desire was clearly to get home as soon as possible after an absence of nearly three years. It is curious to think of the risks supposed to be incurred by passengers on board a merchantman.

The following comment on the colour of the ink is amply borne out in the log: "Poor fellow! to wait from the middle of November to the end of December, and perhaps even longer, it must be sad work; especially in a place where the ink is so abominably pale. What a surprise to him it must have been on October 20th to be visited, collared, and thrust out of the *Peterel* by Captain Inglis. He kindly passes over the poignancy of his feelings in quitting his ship, his officers, and his men.

"What a pity it is that he should not be in England at the time of this promotion, because he certainly would have had an appointment, so everybody says, and therefore it must be right for me to say it too. Had he been really here, the certainty of the appointment, I dare say, would not

THE WAY TO CHURCH FROM PORTSDOWN LODGE
(When the forts were constructed, this avenue was cut down.)

At Home and Abroad

have been half so great ; as it could not be brought to the proof, his absence will be always a lucky source of regret."

The "promotion" spoken of in this letter was extensive, and took place on January 1, 1801, on the occasion of the union of Great Britain and Ireland. At the same time there was an increase in the number of line-of-battle ships which is commented on with reference to Charles.

" Eliza talks of having read in a newspaper that all the 1st lieutenants of the frigates whose captains were to be sent into line-of-battle ships were to be promoted to the rank of commanders. If it be true, Mr. Valentine may afford himself a fine Valentine's knot, and Charles may perhaps become 1st of the *Endymion*, though I suppose Captain Durham is too likely to bring a villain with him under that denomination."

The letters give no account of the homecoming, but from the story of William Price's return in "Mansfield Park," we can see that Jane knew something of the mingled feelings of such a meeting.

"This dear William would soon be amongst them. . . . scarcely ten days had passed since Fanny had been in the agitation of her first dinner visit, when she found herself in an agitation of a higher nature. . . . watching in the hall, in the lobby, on the stairs, for the first sound of the carriage which was to bring her a brother.

Jane Austen's Sailor Brothers

" It was long before Fanny could recover from the agitating happiness of such an hour as was formed by the last thirty minutes of expectation and the first of fruition.

" It was some time even before her happiness could be said to make her happy, before the disappointment inseparable from the alteration of person had vanished, and she could see in him the same William as before, and talk to him as her heart had been yearning to do through many a past year."

CHAPTER VIII

BLOCKADING BOULOGNE

FRANCIS AUSTEN's first appointment on his promotion to post rank was to the *Neptune*, as
Flag-Captain to Admiral James Gambier. It was
not usual for an Admiral to choose as his Flag-
Captain one who had so lately gained the step in
rank. It is clear from the letters of Francis Austen
at this time that he, in common with many officers
in the Navy, was bent on improvements in the
food and general comforts of the crews. Francis
Austen's capacity for detail would here stand him
in good stead. There is one letter of his concerning the best way of preserving cheeses, which is a
good example of his interest in the small things of
his profession. He had, on the advice of Admiral Gambier, made the experiment of coating
some cheeses with whitewash in order to keep
them in good condition in hot weather, and had
found it very successful. He thereupon wrote to
the Admiralty Commissioners recommending that
all cheeses should be so treated before being

Jane Austen's Sailor Brothers

shipped, in order that the men might have "more wholesome and nutritive food," and also "that a material ultimate saving to the public may be effected at an inconsiderable first cost."

We have not far to look for a parallel to this love of detail in the works of Jane Austen. Admirers and detractors are agreed in saying that she thought nothing too unimportant to be of interest, and in allowing the justice of her own description of her work—"the little bit (two inches wide) of ivory on which I work with so fine a brush, as produces little effect after much labour." There is no doubt that naval officers must often have felt in their dealings with the Admiralty that they produced "little effect after much labour."

A curious point of etiquette in connection with these letters is that the Commissioners invariably signed themselves "Your affectionate friends," followed by the names of those concerned in the business.

At the peace of Amiens, Francis Austen, among many other officers, went on half-pay; but when war broke out again in 1803, we find him at Ramsgate, employed in raising a body of "Sea Fencibles." This service was instituted chiefly on the advice of Captain Popham, who had tried something of the same kind in Flanders in 1793.

The object, of course, was to protect the coast from invasion. The corps was composed of fisher-

Blockading Boulogne

men, commanded in each district by an officer in the Navy, whose duty it was to quarter the men on the beach, exercise them, and to have the beaches watched whenever the weather was favourable for the enemy to land. The men were exercised once a week, and were paid at the rate of a shilling a day, with a food allowance when on service.

Captain Austen's report on the coast of the district lying between the North Foreland and Sandown is a document of considerable detail, dealing with the possible landing-places for a hostile army. He comes to the conclusion that in moderate weather a landing might be effected on many parts of this coast, particularly in Pegwell Bay, where "the enemy would have no heights to gain," and, further, "that any time of tide would be equally favourable for the debarkation of troops on this shore." But "in blowing weather, open flat boats filled with troops would doubtless many of them be lost in the surf, while larger vessels could not, from the flatness of the coast, approach sufficiently near." Of course, all is subject to "the enemy's evading our cruisers, and getting past the ships in the Downs."

This time at Ramsgate was of importance to Francis, for it was here that he met, and became engaged to, Mary Gibson, who was his wife for seventeen years. This engagement, though

Jane Austen's Sailor Brothers

" Mrs. F. A." became one of the best loved of
the sisters-in-law, must at the outset have been a
slight shock to Jane and Cassandra, who for long
had been cherishing a hope that Frank would
marry their beloved friend Martha Lloyd. A few
extracts taken from the letters will show their
affection and their hopes.

" I love Martha better than ever, and I mean
to go and see her, if I can, when she gets home. . . .
I shall be very glad to see you at home again, and
then—if we can get Martha—who will be so happy
as we ? . . . I am quite pleased with Martha and
Mrs. Lefroy for wanting the pattern of our caps,
but I am not so well pleased with your giving it
to them. Some wish, some prevailing wish, is
necessary to the animation of everybody's mind,
and in gratifying this you leave them to form some
other which will probably not be half so innocent.
I shall not forget to write to Frank."

The connection of ideas seems very clear. Perhaps it may have been some memory of these old
times, and the wishes of his sister who had passed
away, that induced Francis to make Martha his
second wife in 1828.

That their religious life was the mainspring of
all their actions is sufficiently clear throughout the
whole lives of the two brothers. During this
time at Ramsgate, Francis was noticed as "*the*
officer who knelt in church," and up to the day

Blockading Boulogne

of his death there is one entry never absent from the diary of Charles Austen—" Read the Lessons of the Day."

In May 1804 Captain Francis Austen was appointed to the *Leopard*, the flagship of Rear-Admiral Louis, who held a command in the squadron blockading Napoleon's Boulogne flotilla. This flotilla, begun in 1802, had by 1804 assumed very large proportions. With the object of stirring up the descendants of the Norman conquerors to a new invasion of England, Napoleon, always dramatic in his effects, made a progress through the maritime provinces attended by the Bayeux Tapestry, the display of which was expected to arouse much martial ardour. It was assumed that his great army of veteran soldiers, encamped above the cliffs of Boulogne, was only waiting for favourable weather to embark on board the two thousand flat-bottomed boats. His review of this fleet in August 1804 was, however, so seriously disturbed by one or two of the British men-of-war that the new Emperor was obliged to recognise the impossibility of crossing the Channel unless he had the command of (at least) the narrow seas.

All the naval history that follows, up to the day of Trafalgar, was the outcome of his attempt to obtain this superiority for his " Grand Army of England," The failure of Villeneuve, on his return

Jane Austen's Sailor Brothers

from the West Indies, to reach the appointed rendezvous with Ganteaume off Brest, broke up Napoleon's combination; the army marched to Austerlitz and Vienna, the flotilla was left to decay, and the site of the two years' camp is commemorated only by the Column of Napoleon himself.

The work of watching Boulogne and the neighbouring ports was, in common with all other blockades, as a contemporary writer says, "a trial to the temper, spirits and health of officers and men." There was a strong feeling in England against this system, which seems to have been popular with naval authorities. This opinion is voiced in the following cutting from the *Naval Chronicle* of that date :

"Were it indeed possible to keep so strict a watch on the hostile shores that every effort of the enemy to escape from the ports would be unavailing, that the fortuitous circumstances of calms, fogs, gales, the obscurity of the night, &c., would not in any degree advance his purposes, then would the eventual mischief inseparable from a blockade, by which our marine is threatened, find a compensation in our immediate security. But until this can be effected with a certainty of success, the national interests ought not to be compromised, and our future offensive and defensive means unnecessarily abridged." This extract is perhaps of greater

Blockading Boulogne

interest as an example of the journalese of the
date, than for any unusual depth in the ideas which
it expresses, which merely amount to the fact that
it was considered that the " game was not worth
the candle."

Against this we may set another view of the
blockades as expressed by Dr. Fitchett :

" It was one of the compensations of these
great blockades that they raised the standard of
seamanship and endurance throughout the British
fleets to the highest possible level. The lonely
watches, the sustained vigilance, the remoteness
from all companionship, the long wrestle with the
forces of the sea, the constant watching for battle,
which for English seamen marked those blockades, profoundly affected the character of English
seamanship. When, indeed, has the world seen
such seamen as those of the years preceding
Trafalgar? Hardy, resolute, careless alike of
tempest or of battle ; of frames as enduring as the
oaken decks they trod, and courage as iron as the
guns they worked ; and as familiar with sea-life
and all its chances as though they had been web-
footed.

" If the great blockades hardened the seamanship of-the British fleets, fighting for long months
with the tempests of the open sea, they fatally
enervated the seamanship of the French navy.
The seaman's art under the tri-colour decayed in

the long inaction of blockaded ports. The seaman's spirit drooped. The French navy suffered
curious and fatal loss, not only of nautical skill but
of fighting impulse."

Nelson's comment is opportune : " These
gentlemen are not accustomed to a Gulf of Lyons
gale, which we have buffeted for twenty-one
months, and not carried away a spar."

Captain Austen's idea of the best way to mini-
mise the evils of a blockade was to give the men
as much work to do as possible in the care of the
ship. At one time this took the form of having
the boats re-painted. Over this question we have
the following characteristic letter :

" Leopard, DUNGENESS, June 23, 1804.

" SIR,—I have received your letter of 21st instant, relative to the paint and oil I have demanded
for the preservation of the boats of his Majesty's
ship under my command, and in reply to it beg
leave to inform you that I did not make that
demand without having previously stated to the
Navy Board by letter the situation of the boats of
the *Leopard*, and the necessity of an extra proportion of paint being supplied for them ; and as by
their answer they appeared to have approved of
my application, inasmuch as they told me orders
had been sent to Deal to issue it, I concluded
nothing more remained for me than to demand

Blockading Boulogne

the necessary quantity. Presuming, however, from the tenor of your letter, that you have received no direction on the subject, I shall write to renew my application.

"With respect to 'no colour than white being allowed for boats,' I would only ask you, as knowing something of the King's naval service, how long one of our six-oared cutters would look decent painted all white, and whether a darker colour would not be both more durable and creditable? If, however, such be the regulation of the Board (from which I know there is no appeal), I have only to request, when you receive any order to supply the paint, that you will give an additional quantity of white in lieu of black.

"The paint to which you allude in your letter as having been supplied on the 9th and 12th June, was sea store, and ought to have been furnished to the ship months ago. Nor is it more than sufficient to make her decent and fit for an Admiral to hoist his flag in.

"I am, Sir, your humble servant,
"FRANCIS WM. AUSTEN.

"Geo. Lawrence, Esq., &c., &c."

Shingle ballast was one of the grievances of naval officers at that time. It was, naturally, much cheaper than iron ballast, but it had a particularly awkward habit of shifting, and the larger stones

Jane Austen's Sailor Brothers

occasionally drilled holes in the ship. It was also very bulky and difficult to stow.

Francis Austen was neither slow to enter a protest, nor easily put off his point. He writes:

"Though the ship is deep enough in the water, she can only acquire the proper stability by having the weight placed lower. By a letter which I have this day received from the Navy Board in answer to my request, I am informed that the *Leopard* cannot be supplied with more than the established proportion of iron ballast, but if I wish for more directions shall be given for supplying shingle. I have, therefore, to request you will be pleased to move their Lordships to give directions for the *Leopard's* being supplied with the additional *iron ballast* as requested in my letter to the Navy Board."

About this time Francis Austen began to keep a private note-book, which is still in existence, in which he recorded (not always seriously) points of interest in the places he visited. He seems to have kept this note-book while he was in the *Leopard*, then laid it aside for three years, and begun it again when he was Captain of the *St. Albans.* His notes on the "Anchorage Off Boulogne" contain some interesting details.

"Directions for Sailing into the Roads.—There is no danger whatever in approaching the anchorage usually occupied by the English squadron

Blockading Boulogne

employed at the blockade of Boulogne, as the water is deep and the soundings are regular. There is a bank called the 'Basse du Basse,' which lies about a mile off Ambleteuse, extending in a direction nearly parallel to the shore, but rather diverging outwards to the westward of Boulogne Pier; on it there are in some places as little as three fathoms at low water, and within it considerably deeper water." He goes on with some special advice for the various types of vessel.

"The situation usually occupied by the British squadron off Boulogne is, with the town bearing from S.S.E. to E.S.E., distant about four miles, in from 16 to 20 fathoms water; coarse sandy bottom, with large shells and stones, which would probably injure the cables materially, but that from the depth of water and strength of the tides, little of them can ever drag on the bottom,

"From Cape Grisnez to Portel the coast is little else than one continual battery, and I conceive it to be absolutely impregnable to any attack from the sea. Of its defences towards the land I know nothing. I had no means of knowing anything relative to the landing-places.

"Trade.—On this point I had no means of acquiring any certain information, but believe, previous to the war with England, it was a place of great resort for our smuggling vessels from the Kentish coast. As it is a tide harbour, and completely dry

Jane Austen's Sailor Brothers

at low water, no vessels of very large draught of water can go in, nor anything larger than a boat until nearly half flood."

A hundred years have wrought great changes. The Folkestone and Boulogne steamers have some larger dimensions than the *Leopard* herself, and they go in and out at all states of the tide.

One heading is always devoted to "Inhabitants," and under this Francis Austen remarks: "The inhabitants are French, subjects to Napoleon the First, lately exalted to the Imperial dignity by the unanimous suffrages of himself and his creatures." The sarcastic tone of the reference to Napoleon was characteristic of the general tenor of publications in England at the time. "The Tom Thumb egotism and impudent bulletins of the Corsican usurper continue almost without a parallel in history," says the *Naval Chronicle*. The language in which this protest is couched is hardly that we should use now in speaking of Napoleon.

Charles, when the war broke out again, was reappointed to the *Endymion*, and served on her with some distinction until October 1804, when he was given the command of the *Indian* sloop.

Among other prizes taken under Captain Paget, who finally recommended Lieutenant Charles Austen for command, the *Endymion* had captured the French corvette *Bacchante* on the return voyage from St. Domingo to Brest; she had left

Blockading Boulogne

France about three months before, meeting with the *Endymion* on June 25, 1803. This prize was a remarkably fine corvette, and was added to the British Navy.

Somewhere about this time Charles had come across Lord Leven and his family, and was evidently useful to them in some way, besides being doubtless extremely agreeable. When Lord and Lady Leven were in Bath, they made some effort to become acquainted with the family of Mr. Austen, and Jane writes to Cassandra describing a visit paid one morning by her mother and herself:

"When I tell you I have been visiting a countess this morning, you will immediately (with great justice, but no truth) guess it to be Lady Roden. No; it is Lady Leven, the mother of Lord Balgonie. On receiving a message from Lord and Lady Leven through the Mackys, declaring their intention of waiting on us, we thought it right to go to them. I hope we have not done too much, but friends and admirers of Charles must be attended to. They seem very reasonable, good sort of people, very civil, and full of his praise. We were shown at first into an empty drawing-room, and presently in came his lordship (not knowing who we were) to apologise for the servant's mistake, and to say himself—what was untrue—that Lady Leven was not within. He is a tall, gentleman-like looking man, with spectacles, and rather deaf. After sitting with him ten minutes we walked away, but Lady Leven coming out of the dining-parlour as we passed the door, we were obliged to attend her back to it, and pay our visit over again. She is a stout woman, with a very handsome face. By this means we had the pleasure of hearing Charles's praises twice over. They think themselves excessively obliged to him, and estimate him so highly as to wish Lord Balgonie, when he is quite recovered, to go out to him.

"There is a pretty little Lady Marianne of the party to be shaken hands with, and asked if she remembered Mr. Austen. . . . I shall write to Charles by the next packet, unless you tell me in the meantime of your intending to do it.

"Believe me, if you chuse,

"Your affectionate sister."

In January 1805, just before Francis Austen was moved from the *Leopard* to the *Canopus*, and a few months after Charles had taken command of the *Indian*, a family sorrow came upon them. Jane wrote twice to tell the news to Frank, as the first letter was directed to Dungeness, in the belief that the *Leopard* was there, instead of at Portsmouth.

MRS. AUSTEN

Blockading Boulogne

" GREEN PARK BUILDINGS,
" Monday, *January* 21, 1805.

" MY DEAREST FRANK, — I have melancholy
news to relate, and sincerely feel for your feelings
under the shock of it.   I wish I could better prepare you for it, but, having said so much, your
mind will already foretell the sort of event which
I have to communicate.   Our dear father has
closed his virtuous and happy life in a death
almost as free from suffering as his children could
have wished. He was taken ill on Saturday morning, exactly in the same way as heretofore—an
oppression in the head, with fever, violent tremu-
lousness, and the greatest degree of feebleness.
The same remedy of cupping, which had before
been so successful, was immediately applied to,
but without such happy effects.   The attack was
more violent, and at first he seemed scarcely at all
relieved by the operation.   Towards the evening,
however, he got better, had a tolerable night, and
yesterday morning was so greatly amended as
to get up, join us at breakfast as usual, and walk
about without the help of a stick ; and every
symptom was then so favourable that, when Bowen
saw him at one, he felt sure of his doing perfectly
well.   But as the day advanced all these comfortable appearances gradually changed, the fever
grew stronger than ever, and when Bowen saw
him at ten at night he pronounced his situation

Jane Austen's Sailor Brothers

to be most alarming. At nine this morning he
came again, and by his desire a physician was
called in, Dr. Gibbs. But it was then absolutely
a lost case. Dr. Gibbs said that nothing but a
miracle could save him, and about twenty minutes
after ten he drew his last gasp. Heavy as is the
blow, we can already feel that a thousand comforts remain to us to soften it. Next to that of the
consciousness of his worth and constant preparation for another world, is the remembrance of his
having suffered, comparatively speaking, nothing.
Being quite insensible of his own state, he was
spared all pain of separation, and he went off
almost in his sleep. My mother bears the shock
as well as possible ; she was quite prepared for it,
and feels all the blessing of his being spared a
long illness. My uncle and aunt have been with
us, and show us every imaginable kindness. And
to-morrow we shall, I dare say, have the comfort
of James' presence, as an express has been sent
for him. We write also, of course, to Godmersham
and Brompton. Adieu, my dearest Frank. The
loss of such a parent must be felt, or we should
be brutes. I wish I could give you a better preparation, but it has been impossible.

" Yours ever affectionately,

" J. A."

As this letter was wrongly addressed, it was

Blockading Boulogne

necessary for Jane to write a second one to send direct to Portsmouth.

" GREEN PARK BUILDINGS,
"Tuesday Evening, *January* 22, 1805.

" MY DEAREST FRANK,—I wrote to you yesterday, but your letter to Cassandra this morning, by which we learn the probability of your being by this time at Portsmouth, obliges me to write to you again, having, unfortunately, a communication as necessary as painful to make to you. Your affectionate heart will be greatly wounded, and I wish the shock could have been lessened by a better preparation ; but the event has been sudden, and so must be the information of it. We have lost an excellent father. An illness of only eight and forty hours carried him off yesterday morning between ten and eleven. He was seized on Saturday with a return of the feverish complaint which he had been subject to for the last three years— evidently a more violent attack from the first, as the applications which had before produced almost immediate relief seemed for some time to afford him scarcely any. On Sunday, however, he was much better—so much so as to make Bowen quite easy, and give us every hope of his being well again in a few days. But these hopes gradually gave way as the day advanced, and when Bowen saw him at ten that night he was greatly alarmed. A physician was called in yesterday morning, but he was at that time past all possibility of cure ; and Dr. Gibbs and Mr. Bowen had scarcely left his room before he sunk into a sleep from which he never awoke. Everything, I trust and believe, was done for him that was possible. It has been very sudden. Within twenty-four hours of his death he was walking about with only the help of a stick—was even reading. We had, however, some hours of preparation, and when we understood his recovery to be hopeless, most fervently did we pray for the speedy release which ensued. To have seen him languishing long, struggling for hours, would have been dreadful—and, thank God, we were all spared from it. Except the restlessness and confusion of high fever, he did not suffer, and he was mercifully spared from knowing that he was about to quit objects so beloved and so fondly cherished as his wife and children ever were. His tenderness as a father, who can do justice to ? My mother is tolerably well ; she bears up with the greatest fortitude, but I fear her health must suffer under such a shock. An express was sent for James, and he arrived here this morning before eight o'clock. The funeral is to be on Saturday at Walcot Church. The serenity of the corpse is most delightful. It preserves the sweet, benevolent smile which always distinguished him. They kindly press my mother

Blockading Boulogne

to remove to Steventon as soon as it is all over,
but I do not believe she will leave Bath at present.
We must have this house for three months longer,
and here we shall probably stay till the end of that
time. We all unite in love, and I am
                    " Affectionately yours,
                              " J. A."

This was followed in a few days by another.

" GREEN PARK BUILDINGS,
            " Tuesday, *January* 29, 1805.

" MY DEAREST FRANK,—My mother has found
among our dear father's little personal property
a small astronomical instrument, which she hopes
you will accept for his sake. It is, I believe, a
compass and sun-dial, and is in a black shagreen
case. Would you have it sent to you now—and
with what direction? There is also a pair of
scissors for you. We hope these are articles that
may be useful to you, but we are sure they will
be valuable. I have not time for more.
                    " Yours very affectionately,
                              " J. A."

CHAPTER IX

THE PURSUIT OF VILLENEUVE

For a little over a year Francis Austen was
Flag-Captain in the *Canopus*. This ship, which
had been captured from the French at the Battle
of the Nile, had originally been called *Le Franklin*,
and was one of the best built vessels in the Navy
of that day, carrying eighty guns.

On March 29, 1805, Rear-Admiral Louis
hoisted his flag in the *Canopus*, and soon afterwards became second in command to Nelson.

Perhaps few, even among British captains of
that day, were engaged in search of French fleets
across the Atlantic twice within a twelvemonth,
but the story in the log-book of the *Canopus* for
that year tells of the chase of Villeneuve before
Trafalgar, of the second cruise and of the battle
of St. Domingo, followed by the return voyage to
England with three French line-of-battle ships as
prizes.

The subtle strategy of the Emperor Napoleon,
with the counter-strokes of Nelson and the British

The Pursuit of Villeneuve

Admiralty, have been often described ; but the history of those months, told day by day in the log-book of the *Canopus*, has a freshness of detail which gives reality to such stock phrases as "contrary winds" or "strange sails," and makes one recognise that it was the men at sea who really did the work.

The escape of Villeneuve's fleet from Toulon begins the series of events in 1805 which led up to the Battle of Trafalgar. Napoleon's original plan has since become well known.

Villeneuve was to be joined in the West Indies by the combined fleets under Ganteaume from Brest, and Missiessy from Rochefort. The force thus gathered was to cross the Atlantic, gain possession of the narrow seas by overpowering the Channel fleet, and then the long-threatened invasion of England was to be attempted by the Grand Army, embarked in the Boulogne flotilla.

The plan was so far forward that the fleet from Toulon was already at sea, and the Rochefort squadron had reached the West Indies. It only remained to get the Brest fleet out of harbour. This was, however, exactly where the plan failed. The blockading force was not to be moved and could not be eluded. False news of troubles in India and false declarations of intentions were all unavailing ; and even the bluff in the French papers that, so far from waiting till the British

Jane Austen's Sailor Brothers

would let them go, the French fleet could and would sail whenever it was convenient, did not effect the withdrawal of a single British ship from Ushant. At the same time the fact that the Toulon fleet was at large was enough to cause anxiety to Nelson, especially as it was quite impossible to tell what might be Villeneuve's orders. Nelson supposed him to be making for Egypt, and took up a position accordingly midway between Sardinia and Africa.

The fleet with Nelson at this time is recorded in the log of the *Canopus* as follows :

100	*Victory*	Rt. Honble. Lord Viscount Nelson, K.B., Vice-Admiral of the White, &c. &c.
		Rear-Admiral George Murray, Capt. of the Fleet.
		Captain Thomas Hardy.
100	*Royal Sovereign*	Sir Richard Bickerton, Baronet, Rear-Admiral of the Red.
		Captain John Stuart.
80	*Canopus*	Thomas Louis, Esq., Rear-Admiral of the Blue.
		Captain F. W. Austen.
74	*Superb*	„ Richard G. Keats.
74	*Spencer*	„ Honble. Robert Stopford.
74	*Swiftsure*	„ Mark Robinson.
74	*Belleisle*	„ William Hargood.
74	*Conqueror*	„ Israel Pellew.
74	*Tigre*	„ Benjamin Hallowell.
74	*Leviathan*	„ H. W. Baynton.
74	*Donegal*	„ Pulteney Malcolm.

The *Royal Sovereign* was found unfit to make the voyage across the Atlantic, and went home

ORDER OF BATTLE AND OF SAILING

	NO.	SHIPS' NAMES.			CAPTAINS.	
REPEATING FRIGATES — VAN SQUADRON	1.	*Canopus*	.	.	{ Rear-Admiral Thomas Louis / Captain Francis Wm. Austen	**STARBOARD DIVISION**
	2.					
	3.					
	4.	*Superb*	.	.	Richard Goodwin Keats	
	5.					
	6.	*Victory*	.	.	{ The Commander-in-Chief / Rear-Admiral George Murray / Captain Thomas Hardy	
	7.	*Donegal*	.	.	Pulteney Malcolm	
	8.					
	9.	*Spencer*	.	.	Hon. R. Stopford	
	10.					
REPEATING FRIGATES — CENTRE SQUADRON	1.					
	2.					
	3.	*Tigre* .	.	.	Benjamin Hallowell	
	4.					
	5.	*Royal Sovereign*	.		{ Rear-Admiral Sir Richard Bickerton / Captain John Stuart	
	6.					**LARBOARD DIVISION**
	7.	*Leviathan* .	.	.	Henry Wm. Baynton	
	8.					
	9.					
	10.					
REPEATING FRIGATES — REAR SQUADRON	1.					
	2.					
	3.					
	4.					
	5.					
	6.					
	7.	*Excellent*	.	.	Frank Sotheron	
	8.	*Belleisle*	.	.	William Hargood	
	9.	*Conqueror* .	.		Israel Pellew	
	10.	*Swiftsure*	.	.	Mark Robinson	

To FRANCIS AUSTEN, Esq.
Captain of His Majesty's Ship *Canopus*

Dated on board the
Victory, in PALMA BAY,
March 26, 1805

(Signed)   NELSON AND BRONTE

The Pursuit of Villeneuve

from Lagos in May for thorough repairs, which were so effective that she carried Collingwood's flag into action, before any other of the fleet, at Trafalgar.

The narrative begins at the Bay of Palma in Sardinia, amid general preparations throughout the fleet.

On the 4th of April the Admiral signalled "to prepare for action, as the enemy's fleet from Toulon is at sea." After this the fleet cruised for some days between Sardinia and Sicily, waiting for news of the enemy's movements. If, as was thought possible, they were bound for Egypt, the position taken up by Nelson was a strong one. There were daily consultations of the admirals and captains on board the *Victory*. After about a fortnight of this uncertainty, "intelligence is gained" that the sixteen French ships of the line were spoken on the 7th of April, off Cartagena, going west. On the 18th this news was confirmed, with the addition that they had passed Gibraltar on the 9th, and were joined by five Spanish two-deckers, and had continued westward with fair winds. Now ensued an anxious time. The enemy were well started ten days in advance, with the wind behind them, while the British fleet were still battling with adverse winds in the Mediterranean. Every breeze is carefully noted in the log, and the slow progress evidently gave the greatest concern.

Jane Austen's Sailor Brothers

On the 22nd and 23rd of April, the distance made was only fifteen miles in all : " Extremely variable baffling winds and squally weather, tacking or wearing every two or three hours, the squadron very much dispersed." Ordinarily the *Victory* was within half a mile, "but now four or six miles away." Majorca was in sight at one time, and the African coast at another, but the progress towards Gibraltar must have been scarcely perceptible. The Rock was seen for the first time on the 2nd May, still twelve leagues away, and on the 4th they anchored in Tetuan Bay. Here was hard work to be done in getting fresh water and provisions on board. At Gibraltar on the 6th the *Canopus* did not even anchor, as the wind was at last fair, and their stay was only for four hours.

On May 9th, the *Victory* signalled " to prepare demands to complete provisions for five months," which was accomplished off Lagos in Portugal by the morning of the 11th. Then the Admiral made telegraph signal, " Rendezvous Barbadoes," and the whole fleet made sail for the West Indies.

With fair winds and a straight course, the distance of 3200 miles was accomplished by the 4th of June.

The Pursuit of Villeneuve

The sailing order of the squadron was :

WEATHER LINE.	LEE LINE.	FRIGATES ON VICTORY'S WEATHER BEAM.
100 *Victory.*	80 *Canopus.*	
74 *Superb.*	74 *Leviathan.*	
74 *Donegal.*	74 *Belleisle.*	32 *Amphion.*
74 *Spencer.*	74 *Conqueror.*	38 *Amazon.*
74 *Tigre.*	74 *Swiftsure.*	26 *Decade.*

There is very little in the log to indicate the intense expectation that must have been present as they made their entries of the diminishing distance.

" *May* 15.—Island of Barbadoes S. 64.46 W., dist. 877 leagues.

" *May* 22.—S. 70.15 W., dist. 589 leagues."

The careful comparison of observations with the vessels of the weather line, repairs to spars and sails, and general preparation for what might happen on arrival, seem to fill up the days, while the north-east trade winds gave them fine and clear weather.

" Oh, the wonder of the great trade wind ! All day we sailed and all night, and all the next day, and the next, day after day, the wind always astern and blowing steadily and strong. The schooner sailed herself. There was no pulling and hauling on sheets and tackles, no shifting of top-sails, no work at all for the sailors to do except to steer. At night, when the sun went down, the sheets were slackened ; in the morning when they

135

yielded up the damp of the dew and relaxed, they were pulled tight again—and that was all. Ten knots, twelve knots, eleven knots, varying from time to time, is the speed we are making. And ever out of the north-east the brave wind blows, driving us on our course two hundred and fifty miles between the dawns."

These words, taken from one of our popular modern novels,* give us some idea of what sailing was in those days.

The usual record every twelve hours is " *Victory* north one mile." Sometimes the flagship is rather more distant, and occasionally the "Admiral (Louis) went on board the *Victory*." Doubtless the impatience and excitement was not all on Nelson's part. Every man in the fleet must have felt that a battle was not far off. All this time the three frigates were almost daily out in chase, but no enemy was sighted, and it was not until June 3 that the Admiral signalled that the French and Spanish squadrons were at Martinique, " having gained this intelligence from two English letters of marque."

Next day they arrived at Barbadoes, where the Admiral gave orders to embark troops. Nine regiments had been sent out from England in the spring, but had not arrived in time to prevent Missiessy and his squadron from Rochefort from

* The " Sea Wolf," by Jack London, Heinemann.

The Pursuit of Villeneuve

doing much as they chose during his stay among the islands. His troops had taken possession of Dominica, excepting a fort held by General Prevost's force, and he had laid under contribution Montserrat, Nevis and St. Kitt's.

Missiessy had then departed, according to the Emperor's instructions, for France, crossing Villeneuve's fleet in Mid-Atlantic. Thus Napoleon's grand scheme of combination fell through. The fleets from Toulon and Rochefort missed each other, instead of meeting at the West Indies, and the Brest fleet did not succeed in getting past the British blockade. The *Canopus* log of July 17 records the return of Missiessy's squadron. "Five sail of the line and four frigates arrived at Rochefort, on May 21. Vessels dismantled and remained."

The troops embarked by the squadron at Barbadoes were some of those despatched hither in the spring. There is a record of a characteristic order on June 3 :

"Admiral made telegraph signal—' Troops to be victualled at whole allowance of provisions.'" The practice of the day was that soldiers at sea received smaller rations than the ship's company— just the sort of unreasonable orders which it would delight Nelson to set aside.

Early on the 5th the squadron was again under weigh, the *Victory* leading and the *Canopus* astern;

Jane Austen's Sailor Brothers

but in consequence of wrong information received they were on a southerly course, and hourly increasing their distance from the combined enemy's fleet, which was still among the islands, but to the northward of Martinique. The signal at three o'clock "to prepare for battle" was not to be followed by any immediate action.

On the 7th the Gulf of Paria, in Trinidad, was reached, but still no news of the enemy was obtained. The log merely mentions anchoring there for the night and sailing for the northerly islands next morning. The careful records of barometer and temperature are here interrupted, as "barometer taken down in clearing for action."

All through June 10, 11 and 12 the smaller craft were constantly detached to the various islands for intelligence, and finally they all anchored at Antigua.

"*June* 12.—Admiral made signal to prepare letters for England. At eight o'clock the *Curieux* brig parted company for England."

This brig had a history of some interest. She had been captured from the French on February 3, 1804. She was cut out by the *Centaur* from the harbour of Martinique, just after the Diamond Rock had been seized and garrisoned by the same man-of-war. The story is pathetically told by M. Cheminant, the only French officer who survived the action.

ORDER OF BATTLE AND OF SAILING

NO.	SHIPS' NAMES.			CAPTAINS.
1.	*Canopus*	.	.	{ Rear-Admiral Louis / Captain Francis W. Austen
2.				
3.				
4.	*Superb*	.	.	Richard G. Keats
5.				
6.	*Victory*	.	.	{ Commander-in-Chief / Rear-Admiral Murray / Captain Thomas Hardy
7.	*Donegal*	.	.	Pulteney Malcolm
8.				
9.	*Spencer*	.	.	Hon. R. Stopford
10.				

REPEATING FRIGATES — VAN SQUADRON

STARBOARD DIVISION

NO.	SHIPS' NAMES.			CAPTAINS.
1.				
2.				
3.	*Tigre* .	.	.	Benjamin Hallowell
4.				
5.	*Northumberland* .		.	{ Rear-Admiral Hon. A. Cochrane / Captain George Tobin
6.				
7.	*Leviathan* .		.	Wm. Henry Baynton
8.				
9.				
10.				

REPEATING FRIGATES — CENTRE SQUADRON

NO.	SHIPS' NAMES.			CAPTAINS.
1.				
2.				
3.				
4.				
5.				
6.	*Belleisle*	.	.	William Hargood
7.	*Excellent*	.	.	Israel Pellew
8.	*Swiftsure*	.	.	W. G. Rutherford
9.	*Spartiate*	.	.	Sir Francis Laforey, Bart.
10.				

REPEATING FRIGATES — REAR SQUADRON

LARBOARD DIVISION

To FRANCIS WILLIAM AUSTEN, Esq.
Captain of His Majesty's Ship *Canopus*

Dated on board the *Victory*
in CARLISLE BAY, BARBADOES,
June 5, 1805

(*Signed*)   NELSON AND BRONTE

The Pursuit of Villeneuve

"ON BOARD THE *Curieux*, CAPTURED BY THE ENGLISH,
"*Pluviose* 14, Year 12.

" The only officer remaining of those who com-manded the crew of the *Curieux*, I owe you a faithful report of the cruel tragedy which has delivered us up to the enemy.

" On the 13th instant, before one o'clock in the morning I was on deck with a midshipman and twenty men, according to the orders given by Captain Cordier. The weather was of the darkest, especially in the northern direction. Sentries were placed abaft at the ladder and forward. Our boarding nettings were triced up. We had hardly perceived the English boats before they boarded by the stern and the main shrouds. We had only time to discharge two guns with grape shot, one swivel and a wall piece, when the enemy were on board, and forced us to have recourse to the sabre, pike and musketry."

Lieutenant Bettesworth took a chief part in the attack, and was eventually rewarded with the command of the brig, which had been one of the best vessels of its kind in the French navy.

It was an important mission which was now entrusted to Captain Bettesworth. He was to sail for England with despatches from Lord Nelson for the Admiralty, steering a certain course in the hope that he would sight the enemy's

Jane Austen's Sailor Brothers

fleet. Nelson was right in his conjecture, and Captain Bettesworth reached England with the news that Villeneuve was on the return voyage.

The *Curieux* anchored at Plymouth on July 7, and the Captain reached the Admiralty at 11 P.M. on the 8th, too late, in the officials' opinion, for the First Lord to be disturbed. Lord Barham, a sailor himself, knew well the value of time in naval matters, and was much annoyed at the loss of so many precious hours. Though over eighty years of age his judgment was rapid and accurate. Early on the 9th Admiralty messages were on the way to Portsmouth and Plymouth. Admiral Cornwallis, off Ushant, received his orders on the 11th to detach the squadron blockading Rochefort and send it to join Calder westward off Cape Finisterre, while he himself was to cruise south of Ushant. To the amazement of Napoleon, only eight days after the arrival of the *Curieux*, Sir Robert Calder was ready with fifteen ships off Ferrol. There Villeneuve met him, and an action took place which should have been decisive, but by reason of excessive caution on the part of Calder, only caused loss of ships and men to both sides without advantage to either. Calder joined Cornwallis off Ushant, while Villeneuve went into Vigo Bay and afterwards into Ferrol.

Nelson's squadron began the voyage back from the West Indies on June 15, and we have again

The Pursuit of Villeneuve

in the log of the *Canopus* the matter-of-fact, day-to-day record of routine work, vessels spoken, "no intelligence," small prizes, rigging out of gear, and so forth, behind which was the background of suppressed excitement, of unremitting watch, and of constant readiness. As the months went on and the situation developed, the excitement increased, and reached its climax only with Trafalgar Day.

One entry gives an idea of the difference in the conditions of warfare then and now. "On June 19, an English merchant vessel was spoken by the *Amphion* frigate. They signalled—'Have English papers to the 3rd of May. Interesting debates.' Admiral asked—'Who is First Lord of the Admiralty?' Answer—'Lord Barham.' Knowing so little as they did of affairs at home, they could not be sure that all might not be over before they got back.

"*June* 29.—The *Amazon* at daylight was seen to be towing a captured Spanish *Tartan*, from La Guayra. The people on board did not know of the war." This was undoubtedly an extreme case, and one feels some sympathy for the " people on board," who were captured before they knew that they were fighting.

The winds were naturally less favourable for the return voyage, but by taking a course near Bermuda, and to the Azores, they made much better headway than Villeneuve had managed to do, and

Jane Austen's Sailor Brothers

reached Gibraltar on July 17. After a few days here they gained intelligence of the doings of the *Curieux* brig, and sailed northwards to join Admiral Cornwallis off Ushant.

"*August* 15.—Off Ushant. Lord Nelson saluted Admiral Cornwallis with fifteen guns, returned with thirteen.—Joined the Channel Fleet of twenty-four sail of the line. Answered our signal to follow orders of Admiral Cornwallis in the *Ville de Paris*."

"*August* 16.—Thirty-five sail of the line in company. *Victory* and *Superb* parted company for England."

We read from a contemporary writer that Nelson arrived "filled with mortification, which those who first conversed with him after his arrival state to have amounted almost to anguish, at his disappointment" at having missed Villeneuve in the West Indies.

"*August* 17.—*Ville de Paris* made signal to *Prince of Wales* (Sir R. Calder) to part company, on service previously denoted. Made sail (southwards) in company with squadron of nineteen sail of the line."

"On 20th *Naiad* brought intelligence that the French fleet had sailed from Ferrol on the 13th."

"On·22nd, off Peninsular coast, Admiral Calder signalled 'Prepare for battle.'"

This was almost on the very spot of his inde-

The Pursuit of Villeneuve

cisive fight of July 23. Calder's "order of battle" gives very full details on various contingencies, making a sharp contrast with those signed "Nelson and Bronte," in which the ships' stations only are set down, the rest of the orders being given in the plan of attack well known as the "Nelson Touch."

In the log of 24th "the enemy's fleet of twenty-eight sail of the line were off Cape St. Vincent on the 18th, when they fell in with and destroyed four sail of merchantmen, under convoy of the *Halcyon*, which narrowly escaped capture. In the afternoon, the *Euryalus*, with despatches from V. A. Collingwood, reported that the combined fleet anchored in Cadiz on the 21st, making in all thirty-four sail of the line."

With the enemy in Cadiz the only thing to be done was to wait until they came out. On the 30th the log records: "Joined Vice-Admiral Collingwood's squadron of five sail of the line." The fleet wore and stood off, while *Canopus*, *Spencer*, *Tigre*, *Leviathan* and *Donegal* were ordered to cruise in sight of Cadiz. This plan of keeping a squadron close in shore was followed throughout September, while the fleet awaited the arrival of Nelson from England, and the enemy watched for an opportunity to get out, either to meet the British fleet or to pass them on the way into the Mediterranean.

Jane Austen's Sailor Brothers

An extract from the *Naval Chronicle* shows something of popular feeling in England at this juncture. The remarks on Nelson as contrasted with those of a few months later, after Trafalgar had been fought and won, are more amusing than instructive.

" The arrival of Lord Nelson and Sir Robert Calder's action are the principal events of the last month which have occupied the public mind. It has been said that the former, with Sir Sydney Smith, is soon to embark on some desperate project against the enemy, and we most sincerely wish to see his lordship employed at the present moment in the defence of our own shores. Should the mad project of invasion ever be attempted, the public would feel additional security from having the Hero of the Nile off our own coast. But we greatly lament that ill-judged and over-weening popularity which tends to make another demigod of Lord Nelson at the expense of all other officers in the Service, many of whom possess equal merit and equal abilities and equal gallantry with the noble Admiral.

" Sir Robert Calder has not yet, even to the Admiralty, given that explanation of his conduct which his country expects and his character demands. With his character and its failings we are well acquainted, but we only wish to regard his talents. The French fleet did certainly not

The Pursuit of Villeneuve

run away ; owing to the particular manœuvres of the action, they may be said even to have pursued us, and this may, perhaps, have been occasioned by some feint of our Admiral in order to attack the French to greater advantage. But the whole is at present merely conjecture, until some further explanation of the action has taken place. The account which the French have published in the *Moniteur*, allowing for their natural boasting and vanity, contains a greater portion of truth than usual."

Villeneuve's letter will give an idea of what that account was. " The battle then began almost along the whole line. We fired by the light of the enemy's fire, almost always without seeing them. The fog did not abate during the remainder of the evening. At the first peep of dawn I made signal to bear down upon the enemy, who had taken their position at a great distance, and endeavoured by every possible press of sail to avoid renewing the action. Finding it impossible to force them to an engagement, I thought it my duty not to remove further from the line of my destination."

In consequence of this Sir Robert Calder was recalled and tried by court-martial at Portsmouth in the following December, when he was severely reprimanded for an "error in judgment." The severity of tone of the *Naval Chronicle* towards those who were fighting the country's battles finds its parallel in the French newspapers of the date. Villeneuve was deeply stung by a sneering remark in the *Moniteur* upon what the conduct of the French fleet might be if commanded by a man of ability— so much so as to induce him to disregard Napoleon's wishes that he should go to Toulon, collecting forces on the way, and to lead him to come to close quarters with our fleet as soon as a convenient opportunity offered. Of that opportunity and the Battle of Trafalgar to which it led we will speak in the following chapter.

CHAPTER X

"A MELANCHOLY SITUATION"

THE month of September was spent in blockading Cadiz. The *Canopus*, as already stated, was one of the squadron of five told off to keep close in shore and watch the port. So close were they that one time the *Tigre* nearly ran aground and had to be towed off. The log on September 16th gives an account of what could be seen of the enemy's fleet.

"We stood in till all the enemy's fleet were open of the town, and had an opportunity of distinctly counting them. Their whole force consisted of thirty-three sail of the line and five frigates, all apparently quite ready for sea, with the exception of two ships of the line; one of which (French) had her topmasts struck, and main top-gallant mast down on the deck; the other (Spanish) had her fore-mast struck and fore-stay slack as if doing something to the bowsprit. Of the ships of the line seventeen were French and sixteen Spanish, of which last two were three-

Jane Austen's Sailor Brothers

deckers. The frigates were all French, and one of them appeared to have a poop. We saw also at the Carracas three large ships (two of them appearing to be three-deckers) and two small ones, all of them in a considerable state of forwardness in point of rigging."

On September 28 the *Victory* arrived from England, with Nelson on board, and three days later the *Canopus* joined the main part of the fleet, and was almost immediately told off to take her turn in the duty of fetching water from Gibraltar. The story of the month of October, with its hopes, fears, and disappointments, is best told by Francis Austen himself in the following letter to Mary Gibson :

"*Canopus* AT SEA, OFF GIBRALTAR, *October* 15, 1805.

"MY DEAREST MARY,—Having now got over the hurry and bustle which unavoidably attends every ship while in the act of compleating provisions, water and stores, I think it high time to devote some part of my attention to your amusement, and to be in a state of preparation for any opportunity which may offer of dispatching letters to England. But in order to make myself understood I must endeavour to be methodical, and therefore shall commence the account I have now to send you from the date of my last, which was finished and forwarded by the *Nimble* brig on the

148

" A Melancholy Situation "

2nd of this month. We had then just joined the fleet from the in-shore squadron, and, I believe I mentioned, were about to quit it again for Gibraltar and Tetuan. We sailed that evening with four other ships of the line, a frigate, and five merchant vessels under convoy, and on the following morning fell in with the *Euryalus*, which we had left off Cadiz to watch the enemy. Captain Blackwood informed us by signal that he had received information by a Swedish ship from Cadiz that the troops had all embarked on board the men-of-war, and it was reported they were to sail with the first easterly wind. Though much confidence could not be placed on the accuracy and authenticity of this intelligence, it was, however, of such a nature as to induce Admiral Louis to return with four of the ships to Lord Nelson, leaving the *Zealous* and *Endymion* (both of them crippled ships) to proceed with the convoy to Gibraltar. We rejoined the Commander-in-Chief on the morning of the 5th, and were again dispatched in the course of the day.

" The wind being directly against us, and blowing very strong, we were not able to reach Gibraltar until the 9th, when every exertion was made to get on board such supplies of stores and provisions as we were in want of, and the Rock could supply. This was effected in three days, at which time the wind changed to the westward and became favourable for our watering at Tetuan, where we anchored on the evening of the 12th. We sailed again last night to return to the fleet, having got on board in the course of two days, with our own boats alone, 300 tons of water, and every other ship had got a proportionate quantity. You will judge from this that we have not been idle. We are now expecting a wind to take us out of the Mediterranean again, and hope to accomplish it in the course of the next twenty-four hours; at present it is nearly calm, but appearances indicate an easterly wind. We are, of course, very anxious to get back to the fleet for fear the enemy should be moving, for the idea of their doing so while we are absent is by no means pleasant. Having borne our share in a tedious chace and anxious blockade, it would be mortifying indeed to find ourselves at last thrown out of any share of credit or emolument which would result from an action. Such, I hope, will not be our lot, though, if they do venture out at all, it must happen to some one, as a part of the fleet will be constantly sent in to compleat as fast as the others arrive from having performed that duty.

"Our stay at Gibraltar was not productive of much gaiety to us; we dined only twice on shore, and both times with General Fox, the Governor. We had engagements for several succeeding days

"A Melancholy Situation"

on our hands; but this change of wind making it necessary for us to move off, our friends were left to lament our absence, and eat the fatted calf without us. I believe I have mentioned in a former letter that the young lady *I admired so much* (Miss Smith) was married to the Colonel Keen, whom Sutton will not acknowledge as an acquaintance. As a matter of civility, I called with the Admiral Louis to make them a morning visit, but we were not fortunate enough to find them at home, which, of course, *I* very much regretted. The last evening of our stay at Gibraltar we went, after dining with the General, to see *Othello* performed by some of the officers of the garrison. The theatre is small, but very neatly fitted up; the dresses and scenery appeared good, and I might say the same of the acting could I have seen or heard anything of it; but, although I was honoured with a seat in the Governor's box at the commencement of the performance, yet I did not long profit by it, for one of his aide-de-camps, happening to be married, and his lady happening also to come in during the first scene, I was obliged to resign my situation, happy to have it in my power to accomodate a fair one. The play was *Othello*, and by what I have been able to collect from the opinions of those who were more advantageously situated for seeing and hearing than myself, I did

not experience a very severe loss from my com-
plaisance. I believe the Admiral was not much
better amused than I was, for, at the expiration of
the first act, he proposed departing, which I very
readily agreed to, as I had for some time found
the house insufferably close and hot. I hardly
need add that the evening was not quite so productive of pleasure to me as the last theatrical
representation I had witnessed, which was at
Covent Garden some time in the beginning of
February last, when I had the honour of being
seated by a fair young lady, with whom I became slightly acquainted the preceding year at
Ramsgate.

"Do you happen to recollect anything of the
evening? I think you do, and that you will not
readily forget it.

"*October* 18.—The hopes with which I had
flattered myself of getting out of the Straits two
days ago have not been realised, and, from the
circumstances which have since occurred, it is
very uncertain when we shall get to the fleet
again. The wind on the evening of the 15th
came to the westward and forced us back to
Tetuan, where we remained till yesterday evening,
at which time a frigate came over with orders for
Admiral Louis to give protection to a convoy then
collected at Gibraltar for Malta, as far as Cartagena, after which he is to return to the Com-

"A Melancholy Situation"

mander-in-Chief. We accordingly came over to the Rock this morning, and are now proceeding as fast as possible with the trade to the eastward. Our force consists of five sail of the line and three frigates, which last we shall leave in charge of the convoy as soon as we have seen them safe past the Carthagena squadron. I can't say I much like the prospect. I do not expect to derive any advantage from it, and it puts us completely out of the way in case the enemy should make an attempt to get to sea, which is by no means improbable, if he knows Lord Nelson's force is weakened by the detachment of so many ships. It is since I last wrote to you I believe that your No. 3 has come to hand; it was brought by Brigadier-General Tilson, and was enclosed under cover from Henry. It has been months on the journey. There are still three of yours missing, Nos. 5, 6 and 7, some of which I suppose are gone to seek me in the West Indies, but I trust they will do so in vain there. We have heard from the fleet off Cadiz, and learn that it has been reinforced by the arrival of five men-of-war from England, some of which I hope have brought letters, or they might as well have stayed away. Sir Robert Calder is gone home in the *Prince of Wales*, which I am sorry has happened during our absence, as by it a very fine opportunity of writing has been lost, which is always a source of regret to me when it occurs. I cannot, however, accuse myself of any neglect, and you will, I hope, as readily acquit me of it ; indeed, when you know the circumstances, I am sure you will, though I daresay you will feel rather disappointed to hear a man-of-war has arrived from the Cadiz fleet and find no letter arrived from me, unless you happened to recollect that I expected to go to Gibraltar and, therefore, would probably have been absent when she left the station.

"*October* 21.—We have just bid adieu to the convoy, without attending them quite so far as was originally intended, having this day received intelligence, by a vessel despatched in pursuit of us, that on Saturday, 19th, the enemy's fleet was actually under way, and coming out of Cadiz.

"Our situation is peculiarly unpleasant and distressing, for if they escape Lord Nelson's vigilance and get into the Mediterranean, which is not very likely, we shall be obliged, with our small force, to keep out of their way ; and on the other hand, should an action take place, it must be decided long before we could possibly get down even were the wind fair, which at present it is not. As I have no doubt but the event would be highly honourable to our arms, and be at the same time productive of some good prizes, I shall have to lament our absence on such an occasion on a double account, the loss of pecuniary advantage

"A Melancholy Situation"

as well as of professional credit. And after having
been so many months in a state of constant and
unremitting fag, to be at last cut out by a parcel
of folk just come from their homes, where some
of them were sitting at their ease the greater
part of last war, and the whole of this, till just
now, is particularly hard and annoying.

"You, perhaps, may not feel this so forcibly as
I do, and in your satisfaction at my having avoided
the danger of battle may not much regret my
losing the credit of having contributed to gain a
victory; not so myself!

"I do not profess to like fighting for its own
sake, but if there have been an action with the
combined fleets I shall ever consider the day on
which I sailed from the squadron as the most in-
auspicious one of my life.

"*October* 27, off Tetuan.—Alas! my dearest
Mary, all my fears are but too fully justified.
The fleets have met, and, after a very severe contest, a most decisive victory has been gained by
the English twenty-seven over the enemy's thirty-
three. Seventeen of the ships are taken and one
is burnt; but I am truly sorry to add that this
splendid affair has cost us many lives, and amongst
them the most invaluable one to the nation, that
of our gallant, and ever-to-be-regreted, Commander-in-Chief, Lord Nelson, who was mortally
wounded by a musket shot, and only lived long

enough to know his fleet successful. In a public point of view, I consider his loss as the greatest which could have occurred; nor do I hesitate to say there is not an Admiral on the list so eminently calculated for the command of a fleet as he was. I never heard of his equal, nor do I expect again to see such a man. To the soundest judgment he united prompt decision and speedy execution of his plans; and he possessed in a superior degree the happy talent of making every class of persons pleased with their situation and eager to exert themselves in forwarding the public service. As a national benefit I cannot but rejoice that our arms have been once again successful, but at the same time I cannot help feeling how very unfortunate we have been to be away at such a moment, and, by a fatal combination of unfortunate though unavoidable events, to lose all share in the glory of a day which surpasses all which ever went before, is what I cannot think of with any degree of patience; but, as I cannot write upon that subject without complaining, I will drop it for the present, till time and reflection reconcile me a little more to what I know is now inevitable.

"We arrived off the Rock of Gibraltar two days ago, and having heard of the action as well as that our fleet was in want of assistance to repair their damages and secure their prizes, we pro-ceeded on with a fine, fresh wind at east to run

CAPTAIN F. W. AUSTEN

"A Melancholy Situation"

through the Straits; but before we were out of sight of the garrison the wind chopped round to the westward, directly in our teeth, and came on to blow a very heavy gale of wind, which effectually prevented our proceeding. We bore away for this place and wait a change of wind and weather, not a little anxious for our friends outside, who could have been but ill prepared to encounter such a severe storm as they must have experienced on a lee shore, and probably with crippled masts. Indeed, I hardly expect to hear they have all escaped.

"Off Cadiz, *October* 31.—Having at length effected our escape from the Mediterranean prison and rejoined our friends, I will proceed to such particulars as have come to my ears relative to the action, and present situation of our ships. The object of the enemy was avowedly to get into the Mediterranean, but at the same time they did not, as their conduct proved, wish to avoid a battle, expecting, no doubt, their superiority would have ensured them at least a *drawn* action, and that they would have disabled our fleet so much as to deprive us of the means to prevent their proceeding to Toulon; but in this they were fortunately mistaken. Indeed, they acknowledge that they had considered Lord Nelson's whole force as only twenty-seven, and knowing that he had detached six into the Mediterranean expected to find him with only twenty-one ships, and the irregular mass in which our ships bore down to the attack prevented their counting them, so that till after the action was closed the French Admiral did not discover how great a force he had encountered. The van of our fleet which led the attack have suffered very much, especially the *Victory, Royal Sovereign, Téméraire, Belleisle, Mars,* and *Bellerophon;* but some of the rear vessels hardly got into action at all. Had we been there our station would have been the fifth ship from the van, and I trust we should have had our share.

" The battle was hardly concluded when the weather set in so stormy (and continued so for nearly a week) as to prevent our taking possession of many ships which had surrendered, and of keeping several others. Nineteen are known to have struck; four of which have since got into Cadiz ; three are in our possession ; and the rest, to the number of twelve, are either burnt, sunk, or driven on shore. Of thirteen, which are now in Cadiz, out of their whole force the greatest part have lost nearly all their masts, and are so completely disabled as to make it impossible they can be again ready for service during the winter. On the whole, therefore, we may fairly consider their loss as equal to twenty sail of the line.

" Our ships have been so much dispersed since

"A Melancholy Situation"

the action, by the blowing weather, that Admiral Collingwood has not yet been able to collect reports of their damages or loss; but he has strong reason to hope every ship has been able to keep off the shore, and are now in safety. The action appears in general to have been obstinately contested, and has doubtless been unusually bloody; but it has also been so decisive as to make it improbable the Spaniards or French will again risque a meeting with a British fleet. Had it taken place in the open sea, away from the rocks, shoals, and leeshores there is no doubt but every ship would have been taken, but we engaged them under every disadvantage of situation.

"I was on board the *Euryalus* yesterday, in which ship Admiral Collingwood has his flag at present, and was introduced to the French Admiral Villeneuve, who is a prisoner there. He appears to be about forty-five years of age, of dark complexion, with rather an unmeaning countenance, and has not much the appearance of a gentleman. He is, however, so much of a Frenchman as to bear his misfortunes with cheerfulness.

"I do not yet know in what way we are to be employed, but imagine that, as the *Canopus* is a perfect ship at present, we shall be left with such others as are fit to remain at sea, to watch the enemy in the port; while those ships which have been damaged will go to Gibraltar to refit. Many of them will, I daresay, be sent home, as well because proper masts cannot be procured for them here, as that it will now be unnecessary to keep so large a fleet on this station.

" By the death of Lord Nelson I have again lost all chance of a frigate. I had asked his lordship to appoint me to one when he had the opportunity, and, though I had no positive promise from him, I have reason to believe he would have attended to my wishes. Of Admiral Collingwood I do not know enough to allow of my making a similar request; and not having been in the action I have no claims of service to urge in support of my wishes. I must, therefore, remain in the *Canopus*, though on many accounts I am more than ever anxious to get into a frigate.

" *November* 4.—We have just rejoined the fleet after having been detached to examine the coast and assist distressed ships, and hear the *Euryalus* is to sail very shortly for England with the Admiral's despatches, containing, I presume, the details of the action, with the particular loss of each ship, all of which you will learn from the public papers more correctly than I can possibly relate them, for, indeed, I have as yet learnt scarce anything more than I have already given you.

" I am anxiously expecting letters from England,

" A Melancholy Situation "

and as our last news from Lisbon mentioned four packets being due I hope soon to hear of their arrival, and to be again blessed with the sight of a well-known handwriting, which is always a cordial to my heart, and never surely did I stand more in need of some such support. I yesterday received a letter from Henry, dated the 1st of October, which was brought out by Captain MacKay of the *Scout*, who is an acquaintance of mine, and an intimate friend of my brother Charles. The *Scout* came away on too short a notice to admit of Henry's writing to you or he would have done it. He sends me pleasing accounts of all my family, which is, of course, gratifying to me.

" I must now, my dearest love, bid you farewell, having said all I had got to say. Make my kindest remembrances to all your family at Ramsgate and elsewhere."

Miss Gibson must, indeed, have been hard-hearted if she did not acquit her lover of neglect on receiving such a letter as this while he was on active service. It is written, as was usual, on one large sheet of notepaper, the "envelope," that is the fourth page, full, except where the folds come outside, and the whole crossed in the fine, neat handwriting of the day, very like that of Jane Austen herself.

Jane Austen's Sailor Brothers

The scene in Cadiz Bay, after the action of Trafalgar, can be imagined from the few facts given in the log of the *Canopus* on her arrival from Tetuan.

"*October* 30, at 11, saw a French ship of the line dismasted at the entrance of the harbour. On standing in to reconnoitre the position of the enemy's ship it was judged impossible to bring her out with the wind as it was, and that it was not worth the risque of disabling one of the squadron in an attempt to destroy her. She appeared to be warping fast in, and to have a great length of hawser laid out. The batteries fired several shells over us.

" 31*st.*—Passed the *Juno* and a Spanish 74 at anchor. The Spanish vessel, *San Ildefonso*, had lost all her masts, but was then getting up jury masts.

"At a quarter past four, closed the *Euryalus*, having Vice-Admiral Collingwood's flag, shortened sail and hove to. The Admiral (also the Captain) went on board the *Euryalus*. Several ships at anchor around us.

" A French frigate and brig, with flags of truce, in the squadron.

"At four we had passed the *Ajax, Leviathan*, and *Orion* at anchor, all of them, to appearance, but little damaged in the action. The *Leviathan* was fishing her main yard, and the *Ajax* shifting

" A Melancholy Situation "

her fore-top mast. A large ship, supposed to be the *Téméraire*, was at anchor to the northward of San Luca, with fore and mizen-top masts gone ; and eight others were seen from the masthead to the W.N.W.

"*November* 1.—Saw the wreck of a ship lying on the Marragotes shoal.

"*November* 19.—Saw the *Téméraire*, *Royal Sovereign*, *Tonnant*, *Leviathan*, and *Mars*. These five ships are returning here under jury masts, having suffered considerably in the action of the 21st ult.

" The *Sovereign* was in tow of the *Leviathan*, which seemed to be the most perfect ship of the whole."

The *Canopus*, as Francis Austen foresaw, was left at Cadiz with those ships which had suffered but slightly, as well as those which had shared their own hard fate of being out of the action altogether. Here they stayed till the end of the month, awaiting further developments.

CHAPTER XI

ST. DOMINGO

FRANCIS AUSTEN in the letter to Miss Gibson expresses two wishes, neither of which was to be fulfilled.

He never got into a frigate, as he himself foresaw.

Service in a frigate would have been more exciting, as well as more profitable, than in a ship of the line. The frigates got the intelligence, and secured most prizes.

His other wish, that his letters might seek him in vain in the West Indies, was also not to be gratified, for before two months were over he was again on the passage thither, though whether he had the consolation of meeting his letters is another matter. As this voyage culminated in the action of St. Domingo, and the capture of several valuable prizes, the need for "comfort and support" was certainly not so great as after the disappointment of missing Trafalgar. How great that disappointment was his letter testifies. And some-

St. Domingo

thing must be added to, rather than taken away from, this, in allowing for his natural reserve. From a man of his temperament every word means more than if Charles had been the writer. The fact that the log of the *Canopus*, on the day when the news of Trafalgar was received, is headed "Off Gibraltar, a melancholy situation," is the only indication to be found there of the state of feeling on board. Otherwise, there is nothing but rejoicing in the greatness and completeness of the victory, and sorrow at the death of the Commander-in-Chief.

The account of this second cruise begins with the arrival of Sir John Duckworth.

"*November* 15. *Superb* (Vice-Admiral Sir John Duckworth) and *Powerful* joined company off Cape St. Mary (Portugal).

"Order of sailing :

WEATHER LINE.	LEE LINE.
Superb.	*Canopus.*
Spencer.	*Donegal.*
Agamemnon.	*Powerful.*

"*November* 29.—Saw a man-of-war in the E. N. E. standing towards us ; perceived the stranger had the signal flying to speak with the Admiral, and for having intelligence to communicate. The *Agamemnon* showed her number, and made telegraph signal 'Information of the enemy's squadron. Six sail of the line off Madeira.'

Jane Austen's Sailor Brothers

" Let off rockets to draw the attention of the squadron in the W.N.W.

" Sir Edward Berry came on board, and stated that at eight yesterday evening, Captain Langford of the *Lark* informed him that on the 20th of this month he fell in with a French squadron of six ships of the line, three frigates and two brigs, in Lat. 30 N., Long. 19 W., which chased his convoy to the S.S.E. He escaped by altering his course in the night. Two days after he fell in with the West India outward-bound convoy, and was directed by Captain Lake of the *Topaz* to proceed with the intelligence to the senior officer off Cadiz."

This news was confirmed on December 1, and by the 5th the whole squadron had reached Madeira, only to find, as usual, that the enemy had gone somewhere else. They went on to the Canary Islands, still cruising in search of the French. The entries on December 24 and 25 tell of the meeting with and chase of another squadron, not that which was afterwards engaged at St. Domingo.

"*December* 24, *Arethusa* and convoy met the enemy's squadron which we were in search of on December 16 in Lat. 40, Long. 13. The convoy dispersed, and it is hoped that none were taken. By the last accounts from the Continent, the French had suffered an important check, in which

St. Domingo

8026 were taken beside those killed." This was, of course, an entirely unfounded report, as no severe check had occurred to Napoleon's arms, in fact the great victory of Austerlitz was just won.

"*December* 25, half-past six A.M., saw seven sail in the S.W.; tacked ship and made all sail. Answered signal for a general chace. Perceived the strangers to be vessels of war, and not English. At eight, answered signal to prepare for battle, at nine tacked, at ten cleared the ship for action. Light baffling airs. The strange squadron standing to the southward under all sail; *Superb*, *Spencer*, and *Agamemnon* south, six or seven miles; *Powerful*, N.W., three miles; *Donegal* and *Amethyst*, S.S.W., four or five miles; *Acasta*, E. by S., one mile.

"At sunset the chace just in sight ahead from the top-gallant yard. Our advanced ships S.E. five or six leagues. At six lost sight of all the squadron but the *Donegal* and *Powerful*.

"When the strange sails were first seen, they appeared to be steering to the S.W., and to be a good deal scattered, the nearest being about ten miles from us, and some barely in sight from the deck. They all were seen to make a multiplicity of signals, and it was soon discovered, from their sails, signals, and general appearance, that they were French.

"Their force was five ships of the line and two

frigates. At eight o'clock the weathermost bore down as if to form a line of battle, and, shortly after that, made all sail on the larboard tack. Owing to the baffling and varying winds, and the enemy catching every puff first, we had the mortification of seeing them increase their distance every moment."

It is clear that the escape of this squadron was largely due to the slow sailing of some of these ships. The *Canopus* herself did not sail well in light winds, having been more than two years in commission without docking, and the *Powerful*, a few days afterwards, sprung her foreyard, and had to be detached from the squadron. At the end of the chase, the distance between the leading ship, *Superb*, and the *Donegal*, the last of the squadron, is estimated in James' *Naval History* at forty-five miles.

The squadron then made sail for Barbadoes in order to revictual, and, after coming in for a heavy gale, arrived there on January 12. On the 11th, news was received by a vessel from England, which had been spoken, that Denmark had joined the coalition against France.

It is perhaps noteworthy that the highest records in any of these logs are those during the gale on January 8, 9, and 10, when the *Canopus* attained ten knots per hour, and made six hundred and sixty-one miles in three days.

St. Domingo

Rear-Admiral Cochrane joined the squadron with the *Northumberland*, and acted as second in command to Sir John Duckworth. He had held the same post under Nelson in June 1805, for the few days when the fleet was in West Indian waters.

From Barbadoes they went on to St. Christopher. It is an instance of the difficulties of warfare in the then state of the Navy, that thirteen men took the opportunity of the *Canopus* being anchored close inshore to desert from her, by swimming ashore in the night. No doubt similar trouble was felt on other ships of the squadron.

" On *February* 1, *Kingfisher* brought intelligence that a Danish schooner belonging to Santa Cruz had, on January 25, seen a squadron of French men-of-war, seven of the line and four frigates, in the Mona passage. The master was on board the *Alexandre*, a 74, and the *Brave*, a three-decker, where he was informed they were part of a squadron of ten of the line, and ten frigates and one brig, which had sailed from Brest forty days before, and had separated in crossing the Atlantic.

" *February* 2. At four the *Superb* made signal for the flag-officers of the squadron."

On February 3 this intelligence of the arrival of the enemy at St. Domingo was confirmed, and great must have been the joy thereat.

On February 6 took place the battle of St.

Domingo. The log gives an account which is bare of all detail, except that which is entirely nautical.

"At daylight the frigates ahead six or seven miles.

"Extent of land N.E. by E., and N.W. by W.; nearest part three or four leagues. *Acasta* made signal for one sail W.N.W. at a quarter past six, 'That the strange sail had been observed to fire guns.'

" Half-past six, ' For eight sail W.N.W.'

" A quarter before seven, ' Enemy's ships of war are at anchor.'

" Ten minutes to seven, ' Enemy's ships are getting under way."

" Five minutes before seven, 'Enemy's ships are of the line.'

" At seven, saw eight sail under the land, standing to the westward, under press of sail. Answered signal, ' Prepare for battle.'

" At eight, signal, ' Engage as coming up with the enemy, and take stations for mutual support.'

" Five minutes past eight, ' Make all sail possible, preserving the same order.' Perceived the enemy's force to consist of one three-decker, four two-deckers, two frigates, and a corvette.

" At a quarter past ten, the *Superb* commenced to fire on the enemy's van. At twenty past ten, the *Northumberland* and *Spencer* began firing.

St. Domingo

At half-past, we opened our fire on the first ship in the enemy's line, at that time engaged by the *Spencer*, passing close across her bows, with one broadside brought her masts by the board. Stood on towards the three-decker, firing occasionally at her and two other of the enemy's ships, as we could get our guns to bear. All the squadron in action.

" At a quarter to eleven, the *Atlas* ran on board of us, and carried away our bowsprit, but got clear without doing us material damage.

" At ten minutes to eleven, the dismasted ship struck, as did shortly after two others. Engaged with the three-decker, which appeared to be pushing for the shore. At ten minutes to twelve, gave her a raking broadside, which brought down her mizen mast, and appeared to do great damage to her stern and quarter.

" At twelve o'clock she ran ashore. Wore ship and fired our larboard broadside at the remaining two-decker, which was also making for the shore. At ten past twelve, discontinued the action."

A rather more stirring account of the action is given in a private letter from an officer on board the *Superb*.

This letter also contains the story of the chase of the former squadron on Christmas Day.

" After leaving Lord Collingwood we fell in with a French squadron on December 25, off the

Jane Austen's Sailor Brothers

Canaries, which we now know was commanded by Jerome Bonaparte.

"You cannot conceive the joy expressed by every one on board. Every individual thought himself a king, and expected that day to be one of the happiest Christmases he had ever spent. But from the very bad sailing of several ships of the fleet, Jerome had the good luck to escape, and the joy of the squadron was turned into melancholy, which had not altogether worn off until we found the squadron at St. Domingo (quite a different one). I can give you very little idea of the exultation expressed by every countenance when we were certain of bringing them to action. The scene was truly grand, particularly when you consider the feelings on board the two squadrons, the one making every exertion to get away, and determined to run the gauntlet in order to escape, and the other straining every nerve to prevent their flight. They were at this time going before the wind, and we were endeavouring to cross them, in order to prevent the possibility of their escape, which fortunately, from the superior sailing of the *Superb*, we were able to effect.

"The enemy brought their two largest ships together (*l'Alexandre*, the headmost, and *l'Impériale*) seemingly with a view to quiet the fire of the English Admiral in the *Superb*, before any of the other ships could come up; but in this they were

St. Domingo

disappointed, for the second broadside from the *Superb* fortunately did such execution on board the enemy's headmost ship, *l'Alexandre*, that she became quite unmanageable and lost her station. The three-decker was by this time within pistol-shot of the *Superb*, and apparently reserving her fire for us ; but at this critical moment Admiral Cochrane in the *Northumberland* came up, and notwithstanding the small distance between the *Superb* and *l'Impériale*, he gallantly placed her between us, and received the whole broadside of the largest, and esteemed the finest, ship in the French navy. Several of the shot passed quite through the *Northumberland* into the *Superb*. The action then became general, and, as you must be already informed, terminated most honourably for the British Navy ; for although the enemy was a little inferior, yet, according to the most accurate calculation, they were entirely annihilated in the short space of one hour."

According to the log of the *Canopus*, the time seems to have been nearer two hours than one, but something must be allowed for the enthusiasm of the young officer who writes this letter, and his pride in the very "superior sailing" and other perfections of the *Superb*.

Jerome Bonaparte was not in command of the whole squadron sighted on Christmas Day, but was captain of one of the ships, the *Veteran*. He

Jane Austen's Sailor Brothers

soon became tired of the sea, however, finding the
throne of Westphalia more congenial to his tastes.

The exact comparison between the enemy's force
and that of our own is given in the log.

ENGLISH LINE.			GUNS.	MEN.	FRENCH LINE.		GUNS.	MEN.
Superb	.	.	74	590	Le Diomède	.	80	900
Northumberland		.	74	590	L'Impériale	.	120	1300
Spencer	.	.	74	590	L'Alexandre	.	80	1080
Agamemnon	.	.	64	490	Le Jupitre	.	74	700
Canopus	.	.	80	700	Le Brave	.	74	700
Donegal	.	.	74	590				
Atlas	.	.	74	590				

FRIGATES, &c.

Acasta	.	.	40	320	La Comette	.	40	350
Magicienne	.	.	36	250	La Félicité	.	40	350
Kingfisher	.	.	36	250	La Diligente	.	24	200
Epervier	.	.	16	95				

The following letter was written by Captain
Austen to Mary Gibson on the day after the action:

" *Canopus*, OFF ST. DOMINGO, *February* 7, 1806.

"MY DEAREST MARY,—The news of an action with
an enemy's squadron flies like wildfire in England,
and I have no doubt but you will have heard of
the one we had yesterday soon after the vessel
which goes home shall arrive. It will, therefore, I
am sure, be a source of satisfaction to you and my
other friends at Ramsgate to have proof under my
own hand of my having escaped unhurt from the
conflict. We had intelligence while laying at St.

St. Domingo

Kitts, on the 2nd instant, that a French squadron had arrived at St. Domingo, and immediately quitted that place in pursuit. Happily yesterday morning at daylight we got sight of them at anchor off the town of St. Domingo, consisting of one ship of 120 guns, two of 80, two of 74, and three frigates. Soon as we appeared in view, they got under sail, not to meet, but to avoid us. We had one 80-gun ship, five of 74, and one of 64, besides two frigates and four corvettes. Our situation was such as to prevent their escape. The action commenced at half-past ten, and was finally over by half-past twelve, when three of the enemy's ships were in our possession, and the other two dismasted and on the rocks. The frigates escaped. Had we been two miles farther off the land we should have got the whole. We must, however, be truly thankful for the mercies which have been showed us in effecting such a victory with a comparatively inconsiderable loss. The Admiral is sending the prizes, and such of our own ships as have suffered most, to Jamaica, where, I suppose, we shall follow as soon as we have ascertained that the two ships on shore are in such a state as to prevent their getting off again. I am in hopes this action will be the means of our speedy quitting this country, and perhaps to return to Old England. Oh, how my heart throbs at the idea! The *Canopus* sails so bad that we were nearly the last ship in action ; when we did get up, however, we had our share of it. Our people behaved admirably well, and displayed astonishing coolness during the whole time.

"The first broadside we gave brought our opponent's three masts down at once, and towards the close of the business we also had the satisfaction of giving the three-decker a tickling which knocked all *his sticks* away. We were so intermingled with the enemy that it was impossible to confine our attack to one, and though no one vessel struck to us in particular, I am sure we had a share in each. The Admiral is sending off his despatches, and I have only a few minutes which I have been able to steal from my duty on deck to write these few hurried lines. They will, I trust, be equal to a volume. . . .

"P.S.—We have not suffered much in masts and rigging, and I fancy not an officer is killed in the whole squadron."

The work of repairs had immediately to be considered after the action was over, and no doubt the "duty on deck" was very exacting when Francis Austen managed to snatch time to scrawl this letter for the relief of anxious ones at home.

The end of the two ships which ran on shore is given in the log.

"*February* 9, at eight. Saw the two ships which

St. Domingo

ran on shore during the action of the 6th, appearing to be full of water and quite wrecks.

"Observed the frigates to fire several guns at them. At 9 shortened sail and hove to. The *Epervier* stood towards the wrecks with a flag of truce. *Epervier* made telegraph signal : ' There are about twenty men on board the three-decker, and sixty on board the two-decker. Boats can approach; take them off, and fire the hulls if ordered.'

"Admiral made telegraph signal : ' Send two boats to the *Acasta* to assist in bringing off prisoners.' At a quarter past four, observed the wrecks to be on fire."

Soon after they were all on the passage towards Jamaica.

On February 12, an amusing incident is logged. Amusing it is in our eyes, though perfectly seriously recorded.

" 12. *Acasta* made telegraph signals : An American ship four days from Trinidad. The master reports that he saw there an English gazette, containing particulars of great successes gained by the allied powers on the Continent over the French, who are stated to have been everywhere beaten, their armies destroyed, and Bonaparte flying or killed. This had been brought to Trinidad by the mail boat from Barbadoes, and the garrison fired a night salute on the joyful occasion."

Jane Austen's Sailor Brothers

This was, of course, quite at variance with facts.

The voyage home from Jamaica was uneventful, except for the constant trouble given by *l'Alexandre*, which had evidently been badly damaged in the action, and had at last to be taken in tow. It was a happier home-coming for Captain Austen than he had looked forward to soon after Trafalgar. To return after a successful action with three prizes in company was a better fate than had then seemed possible.

They arrived on April 29, when the record stands :

" Saw the lighthouse of St. Agnes bearing N.N.E. by E., distant six or seven leagues ; made signal for seeing land," with what feelings it is easier to imagine than to describe. Such a description has been attempted over and over again, with varying degrees of success. Jane Austen tells of a sailor's leave-taking and return only once, and then, as is her way, by the simple narration of details. Anne Elliot and Captain Harville are having the time-honoured argument as to the relative strength of the feelings of men and women, and to illustrate his point Captain Harville says : " If I could but make you comprehend what a man suffers when he takes a last look at his wife and children, and watches the boat he has sent them off in, as long as it is in sight, and then turns away and says, ' God knows whether we ever meet

St. Domingo

again.' And then if I could convey to you the glow of his soul when he does see them again; when coming back after a twelvemonths' absence, perhaps, he calculates how soon it be possible to get them there, pretending to deceive himself, and saying, ' They cannot be here till such a day,' but all the while hoping for them twelve hours sooner, and seeing them arrive at last, as if heaven had given them wings, by many hours sooner still. If I could explain to you all this, and all that a man can bear and do, and glories to do for the sake of these treasures of his existence. . ."

Jane Austen must, indeed, have known something of the feelings of "such men as have hearts," and the troubles and joys of the seafaring life.

Several of the West Indian Governments and Trading Associations voted addresses, as well as more substantial recognition, to the Admirals and officers engaged at St. Domingo, who also received the thanks of Parliament on their return to England.

CHAPTER XII

THE CAPE AND ST. HELENA

DURING the cruises of the *Canopus*, we have only
one letter from Jane Austen with any mention of
Frank, and that is before his disappointment of
Trafalgar, or his success at St. Domingo. The
full quotation serves to show some of the difficulties
of correspondence. She writes to Cassandra : " I
have been used very ill this morning. I have
received a letter from Frank which I ought to have
had when Elizabeth and Henry had theirs, and
which in its way from Albany to Godmersham has
been to Dover and Steventon. It was finished
on the 16th, and tells what theirs told before as
to his present situation ; he is in a great hurry to
be married, and I have encouraged him in it, in
the letter which ought to have been an answer to
his. He must think it very strange that I do not
acknowledge the receipt of his, when I speak of
those of the same date to Eliz and Henry, and
to add to my injuries, I forgot to number mine on
the outside." This plan of numbering was a

The Cape and St. Helena

certain safeguard against misunderstandings, as it made it easy to find out if a letter had been lost. The "present situation" was that off Ushant, after the chase of Villeneuve across the Atlantic, and before the orders to return southward had been received.

In July 1806, Francis was married to Mary Gibson, known hereafter by her sisters-in-law as "Mrs. F. A." to distinguish her from the other Mary, "Mrs. J. A."

Among the many social functions subjected to Jane Austen's criticism, it is not likely that the absurdities of a fashionable marriage would escape her attention. The subject is treated with more than ordinary severity in "Mansfield Park"—"It was a very proper wedding. The bride was elegantly dressed, the two bridesmaids were duly inferior, her father gave her away, her mother stood with salts in her hand, expecting to be agitated, her aunt tried to cry, and the service was impressively read by Dr. Grant. Nothing could be objected to, when it came under the discussion of the neighbourhood, except that the carriage which conveyed the bride and bridegroom and Julia from the Church door to Sotherton was the same chaise which Mr. Rushworth had used for a twelvemonth before. In every thing else the etiquette of the day might stand the strictest investigation."

Jane Austen's Sailor Brothers

Such was Jane Austen's comment on the worldly marriage. Her estimate of her own brother's wedding may be better gathered from the account of that of Mr. Knightly and Emma.

" The wedding was very much like other weddings, where the parties have no taste for finery and parade; and Mrs. Elton, from the particulars detailed by her husband, thought it all extremely shabby, and very inferior to her own, 'very little white satin, very few lace veils; a most pitiful business. Selina would stare when she heard of it.' But, in spite of these deficiencies, the wishes, the hopes, the confidence, the predictions of the small band of true friends who witnessed the ceremony were fully answered in the perfect happiness of the union."

From the time of his marriage till the following April, Francis was free to spend his time with his wife at Southampton, where they were settling not far from the house where his mother and sisters now lived.

This time was evidently a very pleasant one for Jane. She makes several mentions of Frank and his wife and their common pursuits in her letters to Cassandra.

" We did not take our walk on Friday, it was too dirty, nor have we yet done it; we may perhaps do something like it to-day, as after seeing Frank skate, which he hopes to do in the meadows by the beach, we are to treat ourselves with a passage over the ferry. It is one of the pleasantest frosts I ever knew, so very quiet. I hope it will last some time longer for Frank's sake, who is quite anxious to get some skating ; he tried yesterday, but it would not do.

"Our acquaintance increase too fast. He was recognised lately by Admiral Bertie, and a few days since arrived the Admiral and his daughter Catherine to wait upon us. There was nothing to like or dislike in either. To the Berties are to be added the Lances, with whose cards we have been endowed, and whose visit Frank and I returned yesterday. They live about a mile and three-quarters from S., to the right of the new road to Portsmouth, and I believe their house is one of those which are to be seen from almost anywhere among the woods on the other side of the Itchen. It is a handsome building, stands high, and in a very beautiful situation."

The next letter is an answer to one from Cassandra delaying her return, evidently a matter of regret to the whole household.

"Frank and Mary cannot at all approve of your not being at home in time to help them in their finishing purchases, and desire me to say that, if you are not, they will be as spiteful as possible, and choose everything in the style most likely to vex you—knives that will not cut, glasses that will not hold, a sofa without a seat, and bookcase without shelves. But I must tell you a story. Mary had for some time had notice from Mrs. Dickson of the intended arrival of a certain Miss Fowler in this place. Miss F. is an intimate friend of Mrs. D., and a good deal known as such to Mary. On Thursday last she called here while we were out. Mary found, on our return, her card with only her name on it, and she had left word that she would call again. The particularity of this made us talk, and, among other conjectures, Frank said in joke, ' I dare say she is staying with the Pearsons.' The connection of the names struck Mary, and she immediately recollected Miss Fowler's having been very intimate with persons so called, and, upon putting everything together, we have scarcely a doubt of her actually being staying with the only family in the place whom we cannot visit.

" What a contretemps !—in the language of France. What an unluckiness !—in that of Madame Duval. The black gentleman has certainly employed one of his menial imps to bring about this complete, though trifling mischief. Miss Fowler has never called again, but we are in daily expectation of it. Miss P. has, of course, given her a proper understanding of the business. It is evident that Miss F. did not expect or wish to have the visit returned, and Francis is quite as

CASSANDRA AUSTEN

The Cape and St. Helena

much on his guard for his wife as we could desire
for her sake or our own."

What the mysterious disagreement with the
Pearson family may have been it is impossible to
tell. That it caused more amusement than heart-
burn is clear, but Jane was always an adept, as
she says herself, at constructing "a smartish letter,
considering the want of materials."

The next we hear of Frank (beyond the fact
that he has "got a very bad cold, for an Austen ;
but it does not disable him from making very nice
fringe for the drawing-room curtains ") is on the
question of his further employment. He was very
anxious indeed to get into a frigate, but feared
that the death of Lord Nelson, who knew of his
desire, would seriously damage his chances of
getting what he wanted. Jane writes : "Frank's
going into Kent depends of course upon his
being unemployed ; but as the First Lord, after
promising Lord Moira that Captain A. should
have the first good frigate that was vacant, has
since given away two or three fine ones, he has no
particular reason to expect an appointment now.
He, however, has scarcely spoken about the
Kentish journey. I have my information chiefly
from her, and she considers her own going thither
as more certain if he should be at sea than if not."
This was in February 1807. Mrs. Frank Austen
was very soon to feel the loneliness of a sailor's

wife. In April 1807, Captain Austen took
command of the *St. Albans*, then moored in Sheer-
ness Harbour.

Naval matters, though much better than they
had been, were by no means in order yet, and
great was the difficulty experienced in getting
the ship properly equipped. Letter after letter
was written by the Captain to "the principal
Officers and Commissioners of His Majesty's
Navy" before the ship could be got ready for
sea, properly supplied with stores and men. It
was not until late in June that they at last got
away on convoying duty to the Cape of Good
Hope.

The account of Simon's Bay in the notebook
of Francis Austen is interesting, when compared with the state of things now existing at
the Cape. After sundry very instructive but
entirely nautical directions for sailing in and out,
and anchoring, he goes on to make a few remarks
respectively on wooding and watering, fortifications
and landing-places, trade and shipping and inhabitants, from each of which we give extracts.

"Wood is not to be had here, except by
purchase, and is extravagantly dear; nor is there
any sort of fuel to be procured.

"Water is plentiful and of an excellent quality;
a stream is brought by pipes to the extremity
of the wharf, where two boats may fill with

The Cape and St. Helena

hoses at the same time, but as the run of water
which supplies it is frequently diverted to other
purposes by the inhabitants, it is rather a tedious
mode of watering, and better calculated for keeping
up the daily consumption after being once completed, than for supplying the wants of a squadron
or ship arriving from a voyage.

"The method generally used by the men-of-war
is to land their casks on the sandy beach on the
N.W. part of the bay, a little to the Westward of
the North battery, where there are two or three
considerable runs of water down the sides of the
mountains, and make wells or dipping-places by
sinking half-casks in the sand. In this way, many
ships fill their water at the same time without at
all interfering with or retarding each other's progress. The casks so filled must be rafted off, as
there is generally too much surf to get them into
the boats, and when the South-easters set in
strong it is impracticable to get them off at all.
The casks may however remain on shore without
injury, and being ready filled may be got off when
the weather suits. Both watering-places are completely commanded by the batteries as well as by
the ships at anchorage.

"The anchorage is protected and commanded
by two batteries and a round tower. One on the
South-east point of the bay, called the Block-
house, on which are three twenty-four-pounders,

and a ten-inch mortar. It is elevated about thirty feet above the level of the sea, and commands the whole of the bay, as well as the passage into the westward of the Roman Rocks.

" The round tower is close at the back of, and indeed may be considered as appertaining to the Block-house. It has one twenty-four-pounder mounted on a traversing carriage, and ¦contains very good barracks for fifty or sixty soldiers. The other, called the North Battery, is, as its name bespeaks, on the north side of the bay. It stands on a small rocky point between two sandy bays, on an elevation of twenty or twenty-five feet above the level of the sea, and is mounted with three long eighteen-pounders and two ten-inch mortars. Neither of these works could make much resistance if regularly attacked by sea or land, and are all completely commanded by higher ground in their rear within half cannon-shot. There is besides these another battery called Tucker's, about half a mile to the southward of the Block-house, but not in sight from the anchorage ; on it are three eighteen-pounders. It was constructed in consequence of a French frigate running into the bay (not knowing it to be in the possession of the English) and getting aground somewhere near that spot. It is however so placed as to be of no use as a defence to the bay, for a ship, or squadron, coming in with hostile intentions need

The Cape and St. Helena

not, except from choice, pass within reach of its guns, and as a military post it is confessedly untenable, being completely commanded by higher ground behind it.

" The only regular landing-place is at the wharf which runs out about fifty yards into the sea, and is very convenient, having always sufficient water to allow of the largest boats when loaded to lie alongside it without taking the ground. In moderate weather, boats may, if required to do so, land in almost any part of the bay, and it is, except where the rocks show themselves, a beach of very fine sand. There is very little trade here, it having been chiefly used whilst in the possession of the Dutch as a kind of half-way house for their ships on their passage both to and from India and China.

" The produce of those countries may however be generally procured, and on reasonable terms, as duties on importation are so moderate that the officers of the East India ships frequently find it worth their while to dispose of their private investments here, rather than carry them to England. There has been a whale fishery lately established by a few individuals in a bay about four miles to the north-east, called Calp's or Calk's Bay, which appears to be doing very well, but I imagine could not be very much extended. There is no ship or vessel whatever belonging to the place, and only a few small boats used for the purposes of fishing.

" The arsenal or naval yard is a compact row of storehouses under one roof, and enclosed with a wall and gates, well situated for its purpose, fronting a sandy beach and adjoining the wharf. It contains all the necessary buildings and accommodations as a depot of naval and victualling stores on a small scale, adequate however to the probable wants of any squadron which is ever likely to be stationed there.

"The inhabitants are a mongrel breed, a mixture of many nations, but principally descended from the first Dutch settlers whose language (probably a good deal corrupted both in ideas and pronunciation) is in general use. The Government is now English, but the civil, as well as the criminal jurisprudence is regulated by the colonial laws, as originally established by the Dutch East India Company, somewhat modified and ameliorated by the milder influence of English law. The prevailing religion is Calvinistic, but there are many Lutherans, and some of various sects."

The contrast between the Cape in 1807 and the Cape in 1905 is so strong that it needs no emphasising.

After calling at Ascension Island and St. Helena, the *St. Albans* returned to England. The progress of contemporary history may be

The Cape and St. Helena

noted by the news which they received on their way back, which was duly logged :

" By this ship informed of capture of Copenhagen and the cession of the Danish fleet to the English forces under Lord Cathcart and Admiral Gambier." By January 1 they were back at Spithead, where they remained till the beginning of February, sailing thence, as was so often the custom, under sealed orders. On opening the sealed packet Captain Austen found that he was directed to accompany the convoy to St. Helena.

The following account of the island is interesting when it is remembered that at that time it was an unimportant spot, not yet associated with memories of Napoleon. The note opens with a colossal sentence !

" This island being in the hands of the English East India Company, and used by it merely as a rendezvous for its homeward-bound fleets, where during time of war they are usually met at stated periods by some King's ship appointed to take them to England, has no trade but such as arises from the sale of those few articles of produce, consisting chiefly in poultry, fruit, and vegetables, which are beyond the consumption of its inhabitants, and a petty traffic carried on by a few shopkeepers, who purchase such articles of India and China goods, as individuals in the Company's ships may have to dispose of, which they retail to the inhabitants and casual visitors at the island.

"The inhabitants are chiefly English, or of English descent, although there is a considerable number of negroes on the island, which with very few exceptions are the property of individuals or of the Company, slavery being tolerated here. It does not however appear that the slaves are or can be treated with that harshness and despotism which has been so justly attributed to the conduct of the land-holders or their managers in the West India Islands, the laws of the Colony not giving any other power to the master than a right to the labour of his slave. He must, to enforce that right, in case a slave prove refractory, apply to the civil power, he having no right to inflict chastisement at his own discretion. This is a wholesome regulation as far as it goes, but slavery however it may be modified is still slavery, and it is much to be regretted that any trace of it should be found to exist in countries dependent on England, or colonised by her subjects. Every person who is above the rank of a common soldier is in some shape or other a trader. A few acres of ground laid out in meadow, or garden ground, will seldom fail to yield as much produce in the year as would purchase the fee-simple of an equal quantity in England, and this from the extravagant price which the wants of the home-

The Cape and St. Helena

ward bound India ships (whose captains and passengers rolling in wealth, and accustomed to profusion, must have supplies cost what they may) enable the islanders to affix to every article they raise. To such an extent had this cause operated, that a couple of acres of potatoes, or a garden of cabbages in a favourable season will provide a decent fortune for a daughter."

The voyage home was uneventful, retarded by masses of floating gulf weed, which continued very thick indeed for over a week.

By the 30th of June the *St. Albans* was back again in the Downs. The little stir consequent in the family life is indicated in Jane's letters, written when she was away from home at Godmersham. "One begins really to expect the *St. Albans* now, and I wish she may come before Henry goes to Cheltenham, it will be so much more convenient to him. He will be very glad if Frank can come to him in London, as his own time is likely to be very precious, but does not depend on it. I shall not forget Charles next week." A few days later she writes : " I am much obliged to you for writing to me on Thursday, and very glad that I owe the pleasure of hearing from you again so soon to such an agreeable cause ; but you will not be surprised, nor perhaps so angry as I should be, to find that Frank's history had reached me before in a letter

Jane Austen's Sailor Brothers

from Henry. We are all very happy to hear of his health and safety, he wants nothing but a good prize to be a perfect character. This scheme to the island is an admirable thing for his wife, she will not feel the delay of his return in such variety." On the 30th : " I give you all joy of Frank's return, which happens in the true sailor way, just after our being told not to expect him for some weeks. The wind had been very much against him, but I suppose he must be in our neighbourhood now by this time. Fanny is in hourly expectation of him here. Mary's visit in the island is probably shortened by this event. Make our kind love and congratulations to her."

While on these last voyages Captain Austen made two charts, one of Simon's Bay, and one of the north-west side of the island of St. Helena, which are still in use at the Admiralty. An interesting point in the correspondence of the Captain of the *St. Albans* at this time relates to the conduct of the masters of the various vessels belonging to the convoy. They are very warmly commended for their skill and attention, while some few from the " cheerfulness and alacrity with which they repeatedly towed for many successive days some heavy sailing ships of the convoy, a service always disagreeable, and often dangerous," are specially recommended to the notice of the East India Company. No doubt such

The Cape and St. Helena

praise from captains of the men-of-war engaged
in convoying, was a useful means of advancement
in the service of the Company, and one which
would be earnestly desired. It is an instance of
the justice and appreciativeness which was a
characteristic of Francis Austen that the master of
the very ship which most retarded the progress of
the convoy comes in for his share of praise,
perhaps even warmer than that given to the more
successful officers. " I cannot conclude without
observing that the indefatigable attention of
Captain Hay of the *Retreat*, in availing himself of
every opportunity to get ahead, and his uncommon
exertions in carrying a great press of sail both
night and day, which the wretched sailing of his
ship, when not in tow, rendered necessary, was
highly meritorious, and I think it my duty to
recommend him to the notice of the Court of
Directors as an officer deserving a better
command."

One incident of interest occurred on the return
voyage, which can perhaps be better dealt with
in another chapter.

CHAPTER XIII

STARS AND STRIPES

On June 20, 1808, on the *St. Albans'* passage towards England, there is an entry in the log : " Exchanged numbers with the *Raven* brig. The brig is from off Lisbon. The French have taken possession of Spain. The Spanish Royal Family are prisoners in France. It is not certainly known where the Rochefort squadron is gone, but supposed into the Mediterranean."

This was the beginning of the Peninsular War, in its results disastrous to Napoleon. Napoleon's calm supposition that he could turn out the King of Spain and put in Joseph Bonaparte at his own pleasure, was formed without reference to the feelings of the people of Spain and Portugal ; and futile as their objections might have been if un-supported, their appeal to England was far-reaching in its consequences. Not only was the seat of war transferred to a country which, with its long sea-coast, was favourable to British arms, but the actual naval gain was very great. Such ships of

Stars and Stripes

the French Navy as had escaped from Trafalgar
were still lying in Cadiz, and had now no course
open to them but surrender, while the Spanish and
Portuguese fleets, on which Napoleon counted,
were of course entirely hostile to him.

The feeling in England over this war was very
strong. Added to the hatred of Napoleon, which
would have made almost any of his actions abhor-
rent, there was a real impulse of generous anger
at the oppression shown in pretending to buy the
nation from its wretched King, in order to estab-
lish a purely arbitrary dominion. At the same
time it was a grave question whether Napoleon,
with his many legions, was to be resisted successfully.

As yet, however, Napoleon had not entered
Spain, and Junot was in command of the French
army in the West of the Peninsula.

Sir Arthur Wellesley was first appointed to
command the British expedition, but England does
not always know her best men, and almost at once
Sir Harry Burrard was despatched to take over
the work. The battle of Vimiera was the first
serious encounter, and, but for the hesitation of
Burrard to follow up his advantage, might have
been decisive.

Sir Hew Dalrymple next day arrived from
England to supersede Burrard, and after some
vacillation, not unnatural under the circumstances,

between the policy of Wellesley and that of Burrard, he prepared to push on, and was met by French proposals of a Convention. The Convention of Cintra secured that the French should evacuate Portugal, leaving for France on board British ships, and as they were determined to take everything with them that they could lay their hands on, this was not a bad arrangement for the French. Such, at least, was the opinion in England, and a court of inquiry soon came to the conclusion that it would have been better to leave the entire matter in the hands of Wellesley, who was first on the scene, and had consequently other qualifications for accurate judgment besides those which his genius gave him.

Napoleon, however, saw very clearly how much harm the battle of Vimiera had done him, and came himself to Spain, enraged at Junot's defeat. The campaign of Sir John Moore, ending at Corunna, is too well known for any description to be necessary. The fact that Napoleon could not have everything his own way was established, and the struggle in the Peninsula went on, until it closed five years later with the capture of San Sebastian.

Some extracts from the log of the *St. Albans* and two letters, tell us of the small share which Francis Austen had in this business. " *St. Albans*, in the English Channel, July 22nd, 1808. Received

Stars and Stripes

on board Brigadier-General Anstruther with his staff and suite. Weighed and made sail, twenty-three sail of transports in company.

"*July* 23.—At a quarter past nine hove to and called the masters of the transports on board by signal. Issued to them a sealed rendezvous."

The transports were bad sailors, so it was not until August 5 that they got away from the English Channel on the passage towards Portugal. On the 12th, off Corunna, news was received from the *Defiance*, which caused a deviation in the route in order to bring Anstruther into touch with Wellesley, who was then near Figuero, just before the battle of Vimiera.

"*August* 16.—Saw a number of ships at anchor in Figuero Roads. At two o'clock Captain Malcolm came on board, and brought instructions for the General as to the disposition of the troops.

"*August* 17.—Sent a boat with despatches for Sir Arthur Wellesley on board the transport sent from Figuero (for this purpose).

"*August* 19.—At anchor off the Burlings. Light airs and cloudy weather. At three o'clock a Portuguese boat came alongside with a messenger having despatches for Brigadier-General Anstruther from Sir Arthur Wellesley. At daylight a very thick fog. At eleven the fog cleared away, weighed and made sail to the southward. At three, anchored off Panago in company, hoisted out all the boats and sent them to disembark the troops. At six, the General and his staff quitted the ship. Light airs and fine weather. All the boats of the fleet employed landing the troops."

The landing went on all night, and was finished next morning.

On Sunday, the 21*st*: "Observed an action between the English and French armies on the heights over Merceira." This was the battle of Vimiera, where Kellerman and Berthier vainly endeavoured to dislodge the British from the crest of the hills.

August 22.—"Sent all the boats on shore to assist in taking off the wounded of our army to the hospital ships. Boats also employed embarking French prisoners on board some of the trans-ports."

August 24.—"On the passage towards Oporto." Thence they went back to England, where on September 2 the French prisoners were discharged at Spithead to the prison ships in the harbour.

Two letters written to the Honble. W. Welles-ley Pole, brother of Sir Arthur Wellesley, give this story in a different form.

"*St. Albans* OFF THE BURLINGS, *August* 18, 1808.

"SIR,—I have to state to you for the information of my Lords Commissioners of the Admiralty, that in consequence of intelligence respecting the

PORTCHESTER CASTLE

(The French prisoners were interned in the neighbouring buildings after the Battle of Vimiera.)

Stars and Stripes

British Army in Portugal, communicated by Captain Hotham, of his Majesty's ship *Defiance*, on the 12th inst. off Corunna, Brigadier-General Anstruther commanding the troops embarked on board the transports under my convoy, requested us not to pass Figuera without affording him an opportunity of obtaining some further intelligence relative to the situation of Lieutenant-General Sir Arthur Wellesley; with this, from existing circumstances, I thought it my duty to comply, although contrary to the strict letter of my orders, and accordingly when round Cape Finisterre, steered for Cape Mondego, off which I arrived at noon on the 16th. The Brigadier-General receiving there orders to proceed along the coast to the southward and join the convoy under his Majesty's ship *Alfred*, whose captain would give him further information respecting the position and operations of the army by which he was to guide his own, I proceeded in consequence thereof with the fleet, and yesterday at 1 P.M. joined the *Alfred* off Phenice.

"At four o'clock, in compliance with the Brigadier-General's wish, I anchored with the transports under the Burlings, to prevent their dispersion, and to await the arrival of directions from the Lieutenant-General, to whom an aide-de-camp was yesterday despatched to announce our arrival, force, and position.

Jane Austen's Sailor Brothers

"One of my convoy, having a detachment of the 2nd battalion of the 52nd Regiment on board, parted company on the night of the 12th instant, and has, I suppose, in compliance with the secret rendezvous I issued on the 23rd of July, proceeded off the Tagus.

"I have the honour to be, Sir,
"Your obedient humble servant,
"FRANCIS WILLIAM AUSTEN."

From the same to the same.

"*St. Albans*, SPITHEAD, *September* 2, 1808.

"SIR,—In my letter to you of the 18th ultimate from off the Burlings forwarded by the *Kangaroo*, I had the honour to announce for the information of my Lords Commissioners of the Admiralty, the arrival of his Majesty's ship *St. Albans*, and the transports under my charge at that anchorage. I have now to state to you, for their Lordships' further information, that the following morning the fleet moved on to the southward, and anchored at 3 P.M. off Paymago, where dispositions were immediately made for disembarking the troops, which was effected in the course of the night. On the 20th, I proceeded with the empty transports, agreeably to the directions I received from Captain Blight, to join the *Alfred* off Merceira, about six miles more to the southward, and anchoring there at noon of the 21st, remaining until the 24th, my boats being all that time employed in landing provisions and stores for the army, and embarking a number of French prisoners and wounded British soldiers on board such of the transports as had been appropriated for their reception.

"On the 24th at noon, in obedience to directions contained in a letter I received the evening before from Admiral Sir Charles Cotton, I put to sea with twenty-nine transports under my convoy, and proceeded with them off Oporto, where I anchored on the evening of the 27th, and remained for twenty-four hours until I had seen all safe over the bar. I then weighed, and, making the best of my way to England, anchored at Spithead at 8 A.M. this day."

The *St. Albans* remained in British waters until March in the following year, for the greater part of the time at Spithead, where, in January 1809, Captain Austen took charge of the disembarkation of the remains of Sir John Moore's army on their arrival from Corunna.

Two of the very few references to public matters which occur in Jane Austen's letters are made concerning Sir John Moore and his army.

"*December* 27, 1808.—The *St. Albans* perhaps may soon be off to help bring home what may remain by this time of our poor army, whose state seems dreadfully critical." "I am sorry to find that Sir J. Moore has a mother living, but, though a very heroic son, he might not be a very necessary one to her happiness. Deacon Morrel may be more to Mrs. Morrel. I wish Sir John had united something of the Christian with the hero in his death. Thank heaven, we have no one to care for particularly among the troops, no one, in fact, nearer to us than Sir John himself. Colonel Maitland is safe and well; his mother and sisters were of course anxious about him, but there is no entering much into the solicitudes of that family."

It was in November of 1808 that Mrs. Edward Austen, the 'Elizabeth' of the letters, died. Great grief was evidently felt by all her husband's family. Jane's letters at the time are full of love and sympathy. Cassandra was staying with her brother, and Frank got a few days' extra leave in order to go there, about a month after the death.

Jane writes to tell his plans.

"*November* 21.

"Your letter, my dear Cassandra, obliges me to write immediately, that you may have the earliest notice of Frank's intending, if possible, to go to Godmersham exactly at the time now fixed for your visit to Goodnestone. He resolved almost directly on the receipt of your former letter to try for an extension of his leave of absence, that he

Stars and Stripes

might be able to go down to you for two days,
but charged me not to give you any notice of it,
on account of the uncertainty of success. Now,
however, I must give it, and now perhaps he may
be giving it himself; for I am just in the hateful
predicament of being obliged to write what I know
will somehow or other be of no use. He meant
to ask for five days more, and if they were granted
to go down by Thursday's night mail, and spend
Friday and Saturday with you; and he considered his chance of success by no means bad.
I hope it will take place as he planned, and that
your arrangements with Goodnestone may admit
of suitable alteration."

During Francis Austen's commands of the
Leopard, Canopus, and *St. Albans*, covering the
eventful years of the Boulogne blockade, and of
Trafalgar, and up to 1810, Charles Austen was
serving on the North American station in
command of the *Indian* sloop. The work to
be done on the coast of the United States was
both arduous and thankless. It consisted mainly
in the enforcement of the right of search for
deserters, and the curtailment of the American
carrying trade, so far as it was considered
illicit.

British war policy had made it necessary to
forbid trading by neutrals between European

countries under the sway of Napoleon, and their
dependencies in other parts of the world.
American ingenuity succeeded in evading this
prohibition by arranging for the discharge and
reshipment of cargoes at some United States
port, en route. The ship would load originally at
a West Indian port with goods for Europe, then
sail to a harbour in Massachusetts (for example),
where the cargo was warehoused, and the vessel
repaired. When ready for sea, the captain got
the same cargo on board again, and departed for
the designated market on this side of the Atlantic.
No wonder that American vessels were so frequently spoken by the *Canopus* and the *St. Albans*,
for in 1806 and the following years nearly all the
carrying trade was done under the Stars and
Stripes. American shipmasters were able to pay
very high wages, and desertions from British men-
of-war were frequent. Our cruisers had to take
strong measures in face of this growing evil, and
finally an American frigate was boarded, and
several of the crew forcibly removed as deserters.
Such action was possible only on account of the
great strength of the British naval force, a
practical blockade of the United States ports
being enforced along the whole Atlantic seaboard.
This had been done in consequence of decisions of
the Admiralty Court against some of the reship-
ments, which were held by the Judges to be

Stars and Stripes

evasions of the actual blockades of hostile ports. The state of tension gradually became acute, but both Governments were so loth to fight that negotiations were on foot for several years before the President of the United States declared war in 1812. In 1809 a settlement seemed to have been reached, and a fleet of six hundred American traders had already got to sea, when it was discovered that the treaty could not be ratified. It was indeed almost impossible for England to alter her policy as regards neutral traders, or to abandon the right of search for deserters, so long as every resource was necessary in the struggle against Napoleon.

Captain Mahan, writing on the "Continental System," puts the matter in a nutshell when he says : "The neutral carrier, pocketing his pride, offered his services to either (combatant) for pay, and the other then regarded him as taking part in the hostilities."

In 1808 the *Indian*, Charles Austen's ship, captured *La Jeune Estelle*, a small privateer, but the work on the North-American station was unprofitable as regards prize-money. In 1810 Charles gained post rank as captain of the *Swiftsure*, flagship to Sir John Warren. The great event of these years for him was his marriage in 1807 with Fanny Palmer, daughter of the Attorney-General of Bermuda.

Jane Austen's Sailor Brothers

In Jane's letters there are constant mentions of him.

"*December* 27.—I must write to Charles next week. You may guess in what extravagant terms of praise Earle Harwood speaks of him. He is looked up to by everybody in all America."

"*January* 10.—Charles's rug will be finished to-day, and sent to-morrow to Frank, to be consigned by him to Mr. Turner's care ; and I am going to send ' Marmion ' out with it—very generous in me, I think." " Marmion " was then just published. She was a great admirer of Scott, and doubtless felt the parting from his latest work, even when making a present of it to Charles. In another of her letters she writes :

" Walter Scott has no business to write novels, especially good ones. It is not fair. He has fame and profits enough as a poet, and ought not to be taking the bread out of other people's mouths. I do not mean to like ' Waverley ' if I can help it, but I fear I must."

We hear one more small piece of news concerning Charles in a letter of Jane's dated January 24, 1809 : " I had the happiness yesterday of a letter from Charles, but I shall say as little about it as possible, because I know that excruciating Henry will have a letter likewise, to make all my intelligence valueless. It was written at Bermuda on the 7th and 10th of December. All were well.

Stars and Stripes

He had taken a small prize in his late cruise—a French schooner laden with sugar; but bad weather parted them, and she had not yet been heard of. His cruise ended December 1st. My September letter was the latest he had received."

We have the sequel to this incident in a letter from Charles to Cassandra, dated from Bermuda on December 24, in which he says:

" I wrote to Jane about a fortnight ago acquainting her with my arrival at this place and of my having captured a little Frenchman, which, I am truly sorry to add, has never reached this port, and, unless she has run to the West Indies, I have lost her—and, what is a real misfortune, the lives of twelve of my people, two of them mids. I confess I have but little hopes of ever hearing of her again. The weather has been so very severe since we captured her. I wish you a merry and happy Xmas, in which Fan joins me, as well as in bespeaking the love of her dear Grandmother and Aunts for our little Cassandra. The October and November mails have not yet reached us, so that I know nothing of you of late. I hope you have been more fortunate in hearing of me. I expect to sail on Tuesday with a small convoy for the island of St. Domingo, and, after seeing them in safety, open sealed orders, which I conclude will direct me to cruise as long as my

Jane Austen's Sailor Brothers

provisions, &c., will allow, which is generally a couple of months. My companion, the *Vesta*, is to be with me again, which I like very much. I don't know of any opportunity of sending this, but shall leave it to take its chance. Tom Fowler is very well, and is growing quite manly. I am interrupted, so conclude this by assuring you how truly I am

" Your affectionate friend

and attached brother,

" CHARLES JNO. AUSTEN."

Charles stayed only five months in the *Swift-sure*. In September 1810 he took command of the *Cleopatra*, and brought her home in the following April, after an absence of six and a half years.

Jane's letters show how gladly the news of " our own particular little brother's " home-coming was welcomed. In an account of an evening party given at the Henry Austens', she tells how she heard that Charles was soon to return. " At half-past seven arrived the musicians in two hackney coaches, and by eight the lordly company began to appear. Among the earliest were George and Mary Cooke, and I spent the greatest part of the evening very pleasantly with them. The drawing-room being soon hotter than we liked, we placed ourselves in the connecting pas-

210

CAPTAIN CHARLES AUSTEN

Stars and Stripes

sage, which was comparatively cool, and gave us all
the advantage of the music at a pleasant distance,
as well as that of the first view of every new
comer.   I was quite surrounded by acquaintances,
especially gentlemen ; and what with Mr. Hamp-
son, Mr. Seymour, Mr. W. Knatchbull, Mr.
Guillemarde, Mr. Cure, a Captain Simpson,
brother to *the* Captain Simpson, besides Mr.
Walter, and Mr. Egerton, in addition to the
Cookes, and Miss Beckford, and Miss Middleton,
I had quite as much upon my hands as I could
do.   This said Captain Simpson told us, on the
authority of some other captain just arrived from
Halifax, that Charles was bringing the *Cleopatra*
home, and that she was by this time probably in
the Channel ; but as Captain S. was certainly in
liquor we must not depend on it.   It must give
one a sort of expectation, however, and will prevent my writing to him any more.   I would rather
he should not reach England till I am at home,
and the Steventon party gone."

A curious time and place to receive such news,
and a still more curious informant according to
the ideas of these days, when men do not appear
at an evening party " in liquor."

In November 1811 Charles was appointed to
the *Namur*, as Flag Captain to his old friend, Sir
Thomas Williams, who was now Commander-in-
Chief at the Nore.

211

CHAPTER XIV

CHINESE MANDARINS

In April 1809 the *St. Albans* was again at sea, this time on a voyage to China convoying East Indiamen.

The first place which Captain Austen describes on this voyage is Port Cornwallis, Prince of Wales Island, or Penang. He writes : " This harbour is formed by Prince of Wales Island (better known by the native name of Pulo Penang, signifying in the Malay language ' Betel-nut Island') and the opposite coast of the Malay Peninsula, from which at the nearest part it is distant about two miles. The approach to it is from the northward, and is neither difficult nor dangerous." After further remarks on the best way of sailing in and anchoring, the notes deal with the more generally interesting facts about the island. It must be remembered that at this time the Malays were giving constant trouble to British ships, by small but very ferocious attacks. "Wood is in the greatest abundance, the whole coast of the Malay

Chinese Mandarins

Peninsula in the vicinity of this harbour being a forest, in which any quantity may be had for the trouble of cutting. Ships of war do not, however, usually procure it in that way, from the danger of introducing sickness amongst their crews by the exposure to the sun, which would be unavoidable. It may be purchased on the island at a reasonable price. Water is plentiful, and it has been generally considered of an excellent quality, and to keep well at sea.

"Buffalo beef may be procured here in any quantity. The meat is generally very coarse, lean, and ill-flavoured. Sheep are rarely to be procured, and never but at a very high price. It should seem to be an animal which the Malays have not got, as all those on the island are imported from Bengal, at a great expense, by individuals for their consumption. Fish is neither plentiful nor particularly good in kind; fruit and vegetables are abundant and excellent. They are of those species usually met with in tropical climates, with some peculiar to the eastern parts of India.

"The fortifications are by no means considerable, consisting in a square fort, situated on the extremity of the point which separates the outer from the inner harbour. It is probably quite sufficient to intimidate the Malays, or repel any attack they could make were they so disposed, but I should think it would be far from difficult for two

or three ships of war to destroy it in a short time.
The whole of the works are in a very dilapidated
state. It is obviously incapable of affording any
protection to the greater part of the town, as an
enemy might land to the northward and destroy
most of the buildings, or lay the inhabitants under
contribution, without being exposed to a single
gun from the fort. To the shipping in the harbour,
indeed, it could give some protection, and that probably was the principal consideration in selecting
the spot which it occupies. There was formerly
a work called (from its shape, I presume) the
Frying-pan Battery, but it is now in a state of ruin,
a great part of it having fallen in. The sea
appears to be gradually washing away the soil
from under its foundations.

"The military force usually kept on the island
consists in a battalion of Sepoys about 600 strong,
and a company of European artillery. I did not
understand that there was any militia or means of
increasing the effective force in case of an attack
or other emergency. The public wharf is built
of wood, is of considerable breadth, and, being
roofed over for its whole length, seems well adapted
for sheltering goods of all sorts, in landing or
shipping off, from the effects of the weather, and
especially from the sun, which is generally very
powerful there. The sides being open admit a
free draught and circulation of air, so that it is

perhaps, during the middle of the day, the coolest place in the town, and as such is resorted to by the Europeans, who make it a kind of Mall or lounging-place.

"Shortly after this island was settled by the English, the trade became considerable, and bid fair to increase, as it was found a very convenient situation for ships to touch at on their voyage between India and China, or any of the islands in the Eastern seas, having many local advantages over Malacca, which had previously been used for that purpose.

" It was also considered favourable for the cultivation of pepper, large plantations of which were made and throve exceedingly. In consequence of the war, however, which has so long desolated Europe, and in its progress gradually shut nearly every port on that continent against British ships and trade, the market for pepper grown here has been much straitened, and is now chiefly confined to China. The pepper plantations having in consequence thereof been found very unprofitable concerns, and in many instances I believe heavy losses, are now much reduced in number and extent; nor, so far as I could learn, has any other species of cultivation been introduced to occupy the soil and give employment to the labour and capital which have been so diverted.

Jane Austen's Sailor Brothers

" Many spots, which had been cleared and produced crops, are now neglected, and, as the progress of vegetation here is exceedingly rapid and luxuriant, are verging fast to their original wild, forest-like state.

" Within the last two or three years attempts have been made by a few gentlemen to introduce the culture of the nutmeg, clove and cinnamon ; several plants have been procured which are in a thriving state, and it is generally thought that the soil and situation will suit them ; but no return can possibly be obtained for the first five or six years, which must effectually prevent any but persons of large capitals embarking in such a concern.

" Many parts of the island would do very well for the growth of rice, but it has been the policy of the Government to discourage that species of husbandry as much as possible, from an idea that it would render the settlement unhealthy ; and as that grain can always be procured in any quantity, and at a very cheap rate, from the Malay coast, the measure of obstructing its cultivation on the island seems to have been a prudent one.

" Timber fit for naval purposes may be procured at several places in the neighbourhood, particularly Pegu and Rangoon on the coast of Aracan, and Siacca on the north-east coast of Sumatra. There are several species of it, most, if not all, of which are considered very durable, particularly

Chinese Mandarins

the teak. Poon and other spars fit for masts and yards may also be had from many parts of the Malay coast at very moderate prices, some of which are of a sufficient size to make a main-mast for a seventy-four-gun ship of a single tree. The wood is considerably heavier than fir, but being also much stronger, masts and yards made of it will admit of being reduced in diameter, and nearly, if not quite, equal to the difference in weight. Ships of considerable burden have at different times been built here; the last and largest was a thirty-six-gun frigate built at the expense of the East India Company, and launched in August 1809.

"It was in contemplation a few years back to construct docks here, and the little island of Jerajah was pointed out as a proper situation.

"Gates for the docks were sent out from England, and a steam-engine for working pumps, as the fall of water would not be sufficient to empty the docks; but nothing has yet been done, and the idea seems to have been given up.

"Having the means of docking ships here would on many occasions be productive of very great convenience as well to the public service as to private individuals. For want thereof any ship requiring to be docked must now go to Bengal, or, if a large one, to Bombay, at a great loss of time and increased expense, especially if trading

to China or into the Eastern Seas, in which case
it certainly would occasion the loss of the season
altogether.

"The population of the island is said to be
about 50,000 souls, but I should think it considerably over-rated at that statement. It is composed
of various nations, Malays, Chinese, Cochin-
Chinese, Siamese, Birmans, Bengalees, Malabars,
Chulians, and most of the nations and castes of
India, with a few Europeans, which last fill
situations under the Government, or are engaged
in mercantile concerns. The languages are as
various as the nations, few of them speaking any
other than that of their own country. It is a
singular fact that more than thirty, totally dis-
tinct from each other, are spoken in the Bazar.
The Government, appointed by the East India
Directors, is entirely independent of the Presi-
dencies. The present Governor is a military
man, having the local rank on the islands of
Colonel in the Company's army, and is Commander-in-Chief of all the troops there.

"As the civil code is in many instances suited
to the peculiar customs and usages of the different
nations composing the population, who are in
general fond of litigation, the office of Chief
Judge is a very arduous and fatiguing one."

The *St. Albans* was sent on to China with the
convoy of East Indiamen, and anchored in the

river of Canton. Various matters kept them
here for more than five months, from September
18, 1809, till March 2, 1810.

The river of Canton had for many years been
infested with pirates, called Ladrones, who
robbed and murdered, devastated the country,
attacked villages, and were even a danger to the
town of Canton itself. In order to hold them in
some measure in check, the Chinese Government
had engaged an English vessel called the *Mercury*
to act against them; and immediately on the
arrival of the *St. Albans*, Francis Austen was
asked if he would consider it consistent with his
duty to give any further help. He replied that,
considering the friendly relations between Britain
and China, he should feel himself quite at liberty
to give what help he could. He stipulated however that he should receive a written application
from the Viceroy of Canton, and also that the
restrictions which the Chinese Government had
imposed on the British ships of war to prohibit
them from passing the Bocca Tigris should be
removed, and every part of the river made free to
them. He pointed out that the Chinese Mandarin
(or war) boats would be suitable for the purpose
of attacking the Ladrones if overhauled, fitted
with European artillery and manned by Europeans, and also that the British ships were of no
manner of use in the river, as they were all much

too large, and moreover all but the *St. Albans* would soon be on their passage home. He also expressed a readiness to wait on the Viceroy in order to talk the matter over.

The appointment was made to meet at the Hoppo's house at two o'clock on November 2 ; and here Captain Austen presented himself, but "after waiting nearly half an hour in a close dirty kind of lobby, exposed to the stare of every blackguard who could squeeze himself into the passage leading to it, and having our noses assailed by a combination of villanous smells, I was informed that the Viceroy had gone away, but that the Hoppo would come and speak to me." This Captain Austen absolutely declined, and retired, leaving word that if the Viceroy wished hereafter to see him, " he would at any time have it in his power to do so by coming to the British factory." He adds : " It is not easy to account for the Viceroy's behaviour, but I am inclined to set it down to the score of imbecility, and a struggle between pride and the conviction of his own inability to arrest the progress of the pirates, in which the former has obtained the victory." His dealings with the Viceroy were, however, by no means at an end. About a month afterwards it was necessary to make a serious complaint to the Chinese Government. Some officers of the *St. Albans* had gone ashore for shooting. One

Chinese Mandarins

of them was attacked by a buffalo, and was only rescued from being gored to death by his friends, who shot the animal. Numerous Chinamen immediately gathered round full of indignation at the slaughter of the brute, and, in spite of the protestations of the Englishmen, and their assertions that they would make full restitution, they were attacked in a most violent manner, and only got away by buying their liberty. Evidently the " very friendly feelings " supposed to be existing between the two governments were not so cordially shared by individuals.

After these two minor troubles, a very difficult matter came before Francis Austen, and his skill and courtesy in dealing with it earned him the unqualified thanks of the East India Company, besides some more substantial recognition. Just when the *St. Albans* and her convoy were prepared to put to sea again, they were informed that the " Chops " would not be granted to them, or the ships allowed to depart. The reason given was that a Chinaman had been killed in the town, and, it was stated, by an Englishman. This was a serious matter to deal with, as the evidence was most difficult to collect—the Chinese were thorough-paced liars—and every day of delay now made it more and more likely that the convoy would encounter bad weather on the way home. The Viceroy insisted that the English officers should themselves discover the offender, while Captain Austen pointed out that they had no means of knowing anything about the matter, even if the culprit were one of their own men, and that the police of Canton were more likely to be successful in discovering the offender. In a letter to Admiral Drury, Commander-in-Chief in India, Francis Austen feelingly remarks: " I need not detail to you, Sir, who are so well aware of them, the difficulties that oppose and retard the discussion of any question with the Chinese from various causes, but especially from the want of efficient means of getting our sentiments properly and faithfully rendered into Chinese, nor the pertinacity with which they adhere to any opinion they have once assumed, or assertion once made, in defiance of justice, equity and common sense. You know them all. But when I reflect upon these obstacles, and the general character of the people, I cannot help feeling in how very arduous a situation I am placed, and what important consequences may result from my conduct." The evidence of the two witnesses was certainly not of a sort to make matters easy for the Committee appointed to examine the question. " One states there was neither noise nor fighting, the other that there was noise and he saw fighting for ten minutes, although not being present at the commencement of it he

Chinese Mandarins

knew not how much longer it might have been going on. Again one of them stated that he knew nothing of the business and was not with the deceased when he was stabbed, and immediately afterwards stated that he saw him stabbed, and was only four cubits from him at the time. One of them states it to be quite dark, and the other that it was moonlight."

In spite of all this, when the insufficiency of the evidence was pointed out to the Mandarins, they, "like true Chinese Mandarins (which designation, perhaps, comprises every bad quality which has disgraced human nature), insisted that, as we must now be clearly convinced that the offender was an Englishman, we could no longer have any pretence for withholding him from justice, and therefore would, of course, give him up to be tried according to the laws of China. A Mandarin is not a reasoning animal, nor ought to be treated as a rational one."

The matter was finally settled by allowing the British ships to depart on condition that there was an inquiry held during the voyage home, the result of which was to be communicated from England to China on the arrival of the *St. Albans* and convoy. This seems a truly Chinese mode of arrangement, but not wholly unsatisfactory, as it was discovered that three of the men on the *Cumberland* (one of the Indiamen) had been engaged in the riot, and carrying arms at the time, so that there was some presumptive evidence for their being the actual perpetrators of the deed. The *St. Albans* was back in England by July, with the convoy, calling at St. Helena on the way.

His long service as midshipman must have made the navigation in the China Seas tolerably familiar to Captain Austen. The points mentioned in this part of the log have a peculiar interest at the moment of writing this chapter (May 1905), when we have all been watching the great drama of the Russian fleet's approach to Japanese waters, followed by their destruction, more complete than that of the vanquished at Trafalgar. Cape Varella, Natuna and Saputa Islands, and the Paracels, are all amongst the log records. Passing the latter group seems to have been always an anxious time, as shoals are frequent northward of Singapore, which town, by the way, had no apparent existence in 1809.

There is a curious correspondence, partly by signal, on the passage down the China Seas :

"*March* 16, 1810.—At 1 p.m. telegraph signal to *Perseverance* (one of the tea-ships of the convoy) : 'Do you know anything of the shoal called the Dogger Bank, and which side would you recommend passing it ?'

Chinese Mandarins

"*Perseverance* answers, 'The shoal is doubtful. I should wish to pass to the eastward of it.'

"At 3 o'clock the *Glatton* (another of the tealaden Indiamen) made signal to speak with us. Shortened sail.

"At 4, Captain Halliburton informed me that the Dogger Bank is by no means doubtful, having himself been in a ship which was aground on it. They found it exceedingly irregular."

The connection of the name with the "untoward incident" of October 1904 and the Russian fleet is a coincidence.

One of the outline sketches which occur in the logs is that of Krakatoa Island, in the Straits of Sunda. This mountain was partially destroyed in 1882 by the immense eruption of volcanic matter, which coloured the sunsets all over the world many months afterwards.

Francis Austen was superseded in the *St. Albans* in September 1810 by his own wish. He naturally wanted a short time without employment to spend with his wife, who had not had much of his society since their marriage.

From December in the same year till May 1811 he was stationed off the coast of France as Flag-Captain to Lord Gambier in the *Caledonia*. After this there was another holiday of about two months, spent with his wife and children in paying visits. Jane's letters speak of their being at Steventon, and of a projected visit to Chawton.

On July 18, 1811, he took command of the *Elephant*, and became again concerned in the Napoleonic wars.

CHAPTER XV

The time of Captain Austen's service in the *Elephant* is divided into three periods. For over a year she was employed with Admiral Young's fleet in the North Sea, which was stationed there to watch Vice-Admiral Missiessy, then at anchor at the mouth of the Scheldt, ready to slip out if occasion offered. The ships under his command had been newly built in Napoleon's great dockyard of Flushing, which was rendered ineffective by the constant British blockade. In the autumn of 1812 the *Elephant* was cruising off the Azores with the *Phœbe* and *Hermes*. The disputes concerning trade had by this time resulted in war with the United States. On this cruise we have the record in the log of the capture of an American privateer, the *Swordfish*.

"*December* 27.—At two, saw a strange sail bearing W. by N. Made the signal to the *Hermes* with a gun. Made all sail in chace. At sunset, chace distant two miles. The chace had all the appearance of an armed vessel.

"28.—Fired several shots at the chace. At five minutes to two perceived her hoist two lights and bring to. At two shortened sail, hove to, boarded, and took possession of the chace, which proved to be the American schooner privateer *Swordfish*, out sixteen days from Boston, armed with twelve six-pounders and eighty-two men. During the chace ten of her guns and several spars were thrown overboard."

After her return to England with the prize and another turn at the Flushing blockade, the *Elephant* was ordered to the Baltic. They were engaged in convoying vast numbers of small vessels through the Sound and the Belt past the coasts of Denmark, which was still under the power of France, and in keeping at a distance such armed craft of the enemy as were dangerous. We find, in these short cruises to and fro, as many as two hundred and fifty or three hundred sail in company, under the charge of three or four men-of-war. An entry in the log on October 10 will show the nature of the work : "A boat from the *Zealous* came with letters for the Admiral, and to say that the galliott chaced yesterday was one which had drifted out of the convoy the preceding night, and was captured in the morning by a row-boat privateer off

A Letter from Jane

Nascoi, which, on the *Zealous'* approach, abandoned her and escaped into Femerin. It appearing on examining the master of the galliott that he never had belonged to the convoy, but had merely joined them off Anholt and continued with them for security sake, without applying for instructions, it was decided to consider the vessel as a recapture, and to take her on to Carlskrona as such. She is called the *Neptunus*, Daniel Sivery, master, belonging to Gottenberg, and bound from that place to Stralsund with a cargo of rice, sugar, coffee, and indigo."

The Island of Anholt, captured in 1809, was a possession of great importance to the English when engaged in this work, on account of its lighthouse, which could signal to the ships of the convoy and keep them all in their places. Of this island Captain Austen had a few words to say which show that its importance lay therein alone. After a lengthy and minute description of the lighthouse and all which appertained to it, he continues : " The garrison at present consists of about three men of a veteran battalion, and a few marine artillery, which form by many degrees the most considerable portion of the population, for, exclusive of the military and their appendages of wives and children, there are but sixteen families on the island, who all reside at the only village on it, near the high ground to

Jane Austen's Sailor Brothers

the westward, and whose principal occupation is fishing, in which they are generally very successful during the summer.

"Antecedent to the war between England and Denmark and the consequent occupation of the island by the English, the Anholters paid a small rent to the proprietor of the soil, who is a Danish nobleman residing at Copenhagen; but at present they are considered and fed as prisoners of war by the English. They are an exceedingly poor people, and seem to enjoy but a small proportion of worldly comfort."

The Island of Rugen, which was another anchoring station for the *Elephant*, was the only portion of the conquests of Gustavus Adolphus which still remained under the Swedish flag. The whole tract of country which he conquered was called Swedish Pomerania, but the mainland districts had lately been occupied by part of Napoleon's army under Marshal Brune.

Of Rugen, Captain Austen writes: "The British ships of war were not supplied with fresh beef and vegetables whilst the *Elephant* was there, and I understood because (though they might have been procured) the price was too great, which may probably be in a great degree owing to the neighbouring part of Pomerania having been last year occupied by the French troops, and having suffered much from the effects of war,

A Letter from Jane

as well as having still large armies in its vicinity, which must of course very materially affect the state of the markets for provisions of all kinds."

While the *Elephant* was employed in this way in convoying small vessels backwards and forwards, great events were going on all round. The southern shores of the Baltic were included this year in the great arena of the battles which preceded the downfall of Napoleon.

Napoleon's day was now nearly over. The retreat, in 1812, from Moscow had shaken his reputation, and Prussia no longer attempted to keep up the disguise of friendly relations with France. The revolt of the Prussian regiments of Napoleon's army gave the signal for a national organisation, and the whole country turned openly against France. The garrisons left in the fortified towns, conquered seven years earlier, were the only remnants of French dominion. Marshal Bernadotte, who had fought for his Emperor at Grezlaw and Wagram, had lately been selected to be Crown Prince of Sweden. His interests were now centred in Sweden, and his great desire was to conquer Norway. That kingdom was ceded in 1814, in exchange for Rugen and the Pomeranian territories, and has been, almost from that date, a source of increasing difficulty to the Crown of Sweden. Bernadotte had asked help towards his project from Napoleon, at the

same time promising to give him reinforcements
for the Russian invasion. This offer was refused,
and Bernadotte remained neutral until he saw
that matters were going against his former sovereign. Now, in 1813, he declared himself an
ally of the Russians and Austrians, and brought
across the Baltic into Swedish Pomerania a contingent of 12,000 men, of whom a considerable
number were convoyed by English men-of-
war.

In the log for May 28, 1813, we read : " Sailed
the *Princess Caroline* and several of the brigs,
with a large fleet of transports, for the Sound.
The transports have 4900 Swedish troops on
board, to be landed in Swedish Pomerania."
These soldiers assisted in the defeat of Marshal
Oudinot, and were among the force which
drove back Napoleon from Leipzig in the next
October, just at the same time that Wellington
had completed the liberation of Spain and
was leading his army through the passes of the
Pyrenees.

It is scarcely remarkable that the signal
asking for news should be so frequently made
from the *Elephant* when such events were in
progress.

A letter from Jane to her brother, written
while all this was going on, must have been
truly refreshing, with its talk of hayfields, and

A Letter from Jane

abundance of cheerful gossip about nothing in particular:

"CHAWTON, *July* 3, 1813.

"MY DEAREST FRANK,—Behold me going to write you as handsome a letter as I can! Wish me good luck. We have had the pleasure of hearing from you lately through Mary, who sent us some of the particulars of yours of June 18 (I think), written off Rugen, and we enter into the delight of your having so good a pilot. Why are you like Queen Elizabeth? Because you know how to chuse wise ministers. Does not this prove you as great a Captain as she was a Queen? This may serve as a riddle for you to put forth among your officers, by way of increasing your proper consequence. It must be a real enjoyment to you, since you are obliged to leave England, to be where you are, seeing something of a new country and one which has been so distinguished as Sweden. You must have great pleasure in it. I hope you may have gone to Carlscroon. Your profession has its *douceurs* to recompense for some of its privations; to an enquiring and observing mind like yours such *douceurs* must be considerable. Gustavus Vasa, and Charles XII., and Cristina and Linneus. Do their ghosts rise up before you? I have a great respect for former Sweden, so zealous as it was for Protestantism. And I have always fancied

Jane Austen's Sailor Brothers

it more like England than other countries ; and, according to the map, many of the names have a strong resemblance to the English. July begins unpleasantly with us, cold and showery, but it is often a baddish month. We had some fine dry weather preceding it, which was very acceptable to the Holders of Hay, and the Masters of Meadows. In general it must have been a good hay-making season. Edward has got in all his in excellent order ; I speak only of Chawton, but here he has better luck than Mr. Middleton ever had in the five years that he was tenant. Good encouragement for him to come again, and I really hope he will do so another year. The pleasure to us of having them here is so great that if we were not the best creatures in the world we should not deserve it. We go on in the most comfortable way, very frequently dining together, and always meeting in some part of every day. Edward is very well, and enjoys himself as thoroughly as any Hampshire-born Austen can desire. Chawton is not thrown away upon him. He talks of making a new garden ; the present is a bad one and ill-situated, near Mr. Papillon's. He means to have the new at the top of the lawn behind his own house. We like to have him proving and strengthening his attachment to the place by making it better. He will soon have all his children about him. Edward, George and Charles

A Letter from Jane

are collected already, and another week brings
Henry and William. It is the custom at Winchester for Georges to come away a fortnight
before the holidays, when they are not to return
any more; for fear they should overstudy themselves just at last, I suppose. Really it is a piece of
dishonourable accommodation to the Master. We
are in hopes of another visit from our true lawful
Henry very soon; he is to be our guest this time.
He is quite well, I am happy to say, and does
not leave it to my pen, I am sure, to communicate
to you the joyful news of his being Deputy Re-
ceiver no longer. It is a promotion which he
thoroughly enjoys, as well he may; the work of
his own mind. He sends you all his own plans
of course. The scheme for Scotland we think an
excellent one both for himself and his nephew.
Upon the whole his spirits are very much recovered. If I may so express myself his mind is
not a mind for affliction; he is too busy, too active,
too sanguine. Sincerely as he was attached to
poor Eliza moreover, and excellently as he behaved to her, he was always so used to be away
from her at times, that her loss is not felt as that
of many a beloved wife might be, especially when
all the circumstances of her long and dreadful
illness are taken into the account. He very long
knew that she must die, and it was indeed a release at last. Our mourning for her is not over,

or we should be putting it on again for Mr. Thomas Leigh, who has just closed a good life at the age of seventy-nine, and must have died the possessor of one of the finest estates in England, and of more worthless nephews and nieces than any other private man in the United Kingdom. We are very anxious to know who will have the living of Adlestrop, and where his excellent sister will find a home for the remainder of her days. As yet she bears his loss with fortitude, but she has always seemed so wrapped up in him that I fear she must feel it dreadfully when the fever of business is over. There is another female sufferer on the occasion to be pitied. Poor Mrs. L. P. (Leigh Perrot) who would now have been mistress of Stoneleigh had there been none of the vile compromise, which in good truth has never been allowed to be of much use to them. It will be a hard trial. Charles' little girls were with us about a month, and had so endeared themselves that we were quite sorry to have them go. They are now all at South End together. Why do I mention that? As if Charles did not write himself. I hate to be spending my time so needlessly, encroaching too upon the rights of others. I wonder whether you happened to see Mr. Blackall's marriage in the papers last January. We did. He was married at Clifton to a Miss Lewis, whose father had been late of Antigua. I should

A Letter from Jane

very much like to know what sort of a woman she is. He was a piece of perfection—noisy perfection—himself, which I always recollect with regard. We had noticed a few months before his succeeding to a College living, the very living which we recollected his talking of, and wishing for ; an exceeding good one, Great Cadbury in Somersetshire. I would wish Miss Lewis to be of a silent turn and rather ignorant, but naturally intelligent and wishing to learn, fond of cold veal pies, green tea in the afternoon, and a green window blind at night.

" You will be glad to hear that every copy of S. and S. is sold,and that it has brought me £140, besides the copyright, if that should ever be of any value. I have now, therefore, written myself into £250, which only makes me long for more. I have something in hand which I hope the credit of P. and P. will sell well, though not half so entertaining, and by the bye shall you object to my mentioning the *Elephant* in it, and two or three other old ships ? I *have* done it, but it shall not stay to make you angry. They are only just mentioned.

" *July* 6.—I have kept open my letter on the chance of what Tuesday's post might furnish in addition, and it furnishes the likelihood of our keeping our neighbours at the Great House some weeks longer than we expected. Mr.

Jane Austen's Sailor Brothers

Scudamore, to whom my brother referred, is very decided as to Godmersham not being fit to be inhabited at present. He talks even of two months being necessary to sweeten it, but if we have warm weather I daresay less will do. My brother will probably go down and sniff at it himself, and receive his rents. The rent-day has been postponed already.

"We shall be gainers by their stay, but the young people in general are disappointed, and therefore could wish it otherwise. Our cousins, Colonel Thomas Austen and Margaretta, are going as aide-de-camps to Ireland; and Lord Whitworth goes in their train as Lord-Lieutenant; good appointments for each. I hope you continue well and brush your hair, but not all off.

"Yours very affectionately,

"J. A."

The "something in hand" in this letter was "Mansfield Park." The mentions of ships occur in one of the scenes at Portsmouth, when the whole of the Price family are full of the *Thrush* going out of harbour, and have no eyes or ears for Fanny, who has just come home after an absence of seven or eight years. The scene is worth quoting almost *in extenso :*

"Fanny was all agitation and flutter—all hope and apprehension. The moment they stopped,

238

A Letter from Jane

a trollopy-looking maid-servant, seemingly in waiting for them at the door, stepped forward, and, more intent on telling the news than giving them any help, immediately began with—'The *Thrush* is gone out of harbour, please, sir, and one of the officers has been to——' She was interrupted by a fine tall boy of eleven years old, who, rushing out of the house, pushed the maid aside, and while William was opening the chaise-door himself, called out, ' You are just in time. We have been looking for you this half-hour. The *Thrush* went out of harbour this morning. I saw her. It was a beautiful sight. And they think she will have her orders in a day or two. And Mr. Campbell was here at four o'clock to ask for you ; he has got one of the *Thrush's* boats, and is going off to her at six, and hoped you would be here in time to go with him.'

" A stare or two at Fanny, as William helped her out of the carriage, was all the voluntary notice which this brother bestowed ; but he made no objection to her kissing him, though still engaged in detailing farther particulars of the *Thrush's* going out of harbour, in which he had a strong right of interest, being to commence his career of seamanship in her at this very time.

" Another moment, and Fanny was in the passage and in her mother's arms. She was then taken into a small parlour. Her mother was gone

Jane Austen's Sailor Brothers

again to the street-door to welcome William. ' Oh,
my dear William, how glad I am to see you! But
have you heard about the *Thrush?* She is gone
out of harbour already, three days before we had
any thought of it; and I do not know what I am
to do about Sam's things; they will never be
ready in time; for she may have her orders to-
morrow perhaps. It takes me quite unawares.
And now you must be off to Spithead, too.
Campbell has been here quite in a worry about
you; and now what shall we do? I thought to
have had such a comfortable evening with you,
and now everything comes upon me at once.'

" Her son answered cheerfully, telling her that
everything was always for the best, and making
light of his own inconvenience in being obliged
to hurry away so soon.

" ' To be sure, I had much rather she had stayed
in harbour, that I might have sat a few hours with
you in comfort, but as there is a boat ashore I
had better go off at once, and there is no help for
it. Whereabouts does the *Thrush* lie at Spithead? Near the *Canopus?* But, no matter—
here is Fanny in the parlour, and why should we
stay in the passage? Come, mother, you have
hardly looked at your own dear Fanny yet.'

" Lastly, in walked Mr. Price himself, his own
loud voice preceding him, as, with something of
an oath kind, he kicked away his son's portman-

A Letter from Jane

teau and his daughter's bandbox in the passage
and called out for a candle; no candle was
brought, however, and he walked into the room.

"Fanny, with doubting feelings, had risen to
meet him, but sank down on finding herself
undistinguished in the dusk, and unthought of.
With a friendly shake of his son's hand, and an
eager voice, he instantly began—' Ha! welcome
back, my boy. Glad to see you. Have you heard
the news? The *Thrush* went out of harbour
this morning. Sharp is the word, you see. By
G——, you are just in time. The doctor has
been inquiring for you; he has got one of the
boats, and is to be off for Spithead by six, so you
had better go with him. I have been to Turner's
about your mess; it is all in a way to be done.
I should not wonder if you had your orders to-
morrow; but you cannot sail in this wind, if you
are to cruise to the westward with the *Elephant*.
By G——, I wish you may. But old Scholey
was saying, just now, that he thought you would
be sent first by Texel. Well, well, we are ready,
whatever happens. But, by G——, you lost a
fine sight by not being here in the morning to see
the *Thrush* go out of harbour. I would not have
been out of the way for a thousand pounds. Old
Scholey ran in at breakfast-time, to say she had
slipped her moorings and was coming out. I
iumped up, and made but two steps to the plat-

Jane Austen's Sailor Brothers

form. If ever there was a perfect beauty afloat, she is one ; and there she lies at Spithead, and anybody in England would take her for an eight-and-twenty. I was upon the platforms two hours this afternoon looking at her. She lies close to the *Endymion*, between her and the *Cleopatra* just to the eastward of the sheer hulk.' 'Ha!' cried William, 'that's just where I should have put her myself. It's the best berth at Spithead. But here is my sister, sir ; here is Fanny,' turning and leading her forward ; 'it is so dark you did not see her.' With an acknowledgment that he had quite forgot her, Mr. Price now received his daughter, and having given her a cordial hug, and observed that she was 'grown into a woman, and he supposed would be wanting a husband soon, seemed very much inclined to forget her again."

The statement in the beginning of " Mansfield Park " that " Miss Frances (Mrs. Price) married, in the common phrase, to 'disoblige her family,' and by fixing on a lieutenant of marines, without education, fortune or connections, did it very thoroughly," is not difficult to believe.

CHAPTER XVI

ANOTHER LETTER FROM JANE

UNFORTUNATELY we have not got Frank's reply to his sister's letter, but we have her next letter to him dated about two months later, when she was staying with Edward.

"GODMERSHAM PARK, *September* 25, 1813.

" MY DEAREST FRANK,—The 11th of this month brought me your letter, and I assure you I thought it very well worth its two and three-pence. I am very much obliged to you for filling me so long a sheet of paper ; you are a good one to traffic with in that way, you pay most liberally ; my letter was a scratch of a note compared to yours, and then you write so even, so clear, both in style and penmanship, so much to the point, and give so much intelligence, that it is enough to kill one. I am sorry Sweden is so poor, and my riddle so bad. The idea of a fashionable bathing-place in Mecklenberg ! How can people pretend to be fashionable or to bathe out of England? Rostock market makes one's mouth water; our cheapest butcher's meat is double the price of theirs; nothing under nine-pence all this summer, and I believe upon recollection nothing under ten-pence. Bread has sunk and is likely to sink more, which we hope may make meat sink too. But I have no occasion to think of the price of bread or of meat where I am now; let me shake off vulgar cares and conform to the happy indifference of East Kent wealth. I wonder whether you and the King of Sweden knew that I was to come to Godmersham with my brother. Yes, I suppose you have received due notice of it by some means or other. I have not been here these four years, so I am sure the event deserves to be talked of before and behind, as well as in the middle. We left Chawton on the 14th, spent two entire days in town, and arrived here on the 17th. My brother, Fanny, Lizzie, Marianne, and I composed this division of the family, and filled his carriage inside and out. Two post-chaises, under the escort of George, conveyed eight more across the country, the chair brought two, two others came on horseback, and the rest by coach, and so, by one means or another, we all are removed. It puts me in remind of St. Paul's shipwreck, when all are said, by different means, to reach the shore in safety. I left my mother, Cassandra, and Martha well, and have had good accounts of them since. At present

Another Letter from Jane

they are quite alone, but they are going to be visited by Mrs. Heathcote and Miss Bigg, and to have a few days of Henry's company likewise.

"I expect to be here about two months, Edward is to be in Hampshire again in November, and will take me back. I shall be sorry to be in Kent so long without seeing Mary, but I am afraid it must be so. She has very kindly invited me to Deal, but is aware of the great improbability of my being able to get there. It would be a great pleasure to me to see Mary Jane again too, and her brothers, new and old. Charles and his family I *do* hope to see; they are coming here for a week in October. We were accommodated in Henrietta Street. Henry was so good as to find room for his three nieces and myself in his house. Edward slept at a hotel in the next street. No. 10 is made very comfortable with cleaning and painting, and the Sloane Street furniture. The front room upstairs is an excellent dining and common sitting parlour, and the smaller one behind will sufficiently answer his purpose as a drawing-room. He has no intention of giving large parties of any kind. His plans are all for the comfort of his friends and himself. Madame Bigeon and her daughter have a lodging in his neighbourhood, and come to him as often as he likes, or as they like. Madame B. always markets for him, as she used to do, and, upon our

Jane Austen's Sailor Brothers

being in the house, was constantly there to do the work. She is wonderfully recovered from the severity of her asthmatic complaint. Of our three evenings in town, one was spent at the Lyceum, and another at Covent Garden. "The Clandestine Marriage" was the most respectable of the performances, the rest were sing-song and trumpery; but it did very well for Lizzy and Marianne, who were indeed delighted, but I wanted better acting. There was no actor worth naming. I believe the theatres are thought at a very low ebb at present. Henry has probably sent you his own account of his visit in Scotland. I wish he had had more time, and could have gone further north, and deviated to the lakes in his way back; but what he was able to do seems to have afforded him great enjoyment, and he met with scenes of higher beauty in Roxburghshire than I had supposed the South of Scotland possessed. Our nephew's gratification was less keen than our brother's. Edward is no enthusiast in the beauties of nature. His enthusiasm is for the sports of the field only. He is a very promising and pleasing young man however, upon the whole, behaves with great propriety to his father, and great kindness to his brothers and sisters, and we must forgive his thinking more of grouse and partridges than lakes and mountains. He and George are out every morning either shooting or with the harriers.

Another Letter from Jane

They are good shots. Just at present I am mistress and miss altogether here, Fanny being gone to Goodnestone for a day or two, to attend the famous fair, which makes its yearly distribution of gold paper and coloured persian through all the family connections. In this house there is a constant succession of small events, somebody is always going or coming; this morning we had Edward Bridges unexpectedly to breakfast with us, on his way from Ramsgate, where is his wife, to Lenham, where is his church, and to-morrow he dines and sleeps here on his return. They have been all the summer at Ramsgate for her health; she is a poor honey—the sort of woman who gives me the idea of being determined never to be well and who likes her spasms and nervousness, and the consequence they give her, better than anything else. This is an ill-natured statement to send all over the Baltic. The Mr. Knatchbulls, dear Mrs. Knight's brothers, dined here the other day. They came from the Friars, which is still on their hands. The elder made many inquiries after you. Mr. Sherer is quite a new Mr. Sherer to me; I heard him for the first time last Sunday, and he gave us an excellent sermon, a little too eager sometimes in his delivery, but that is to me a better extreme than the want of animation, especially when it evidently comes from the heart, as in him. The clerk is as much like you as ever.

Jane Austen's Sailor Brothers

I am always glad to see him on that account But the Sherers are going away. He has a bad curate at Westwell, whom he can eject only by residing there himself. He goes nominally for three years, and a Mr. Paget is to have the curacy of Godmersham; a married man, with a very musical wife, which I hope may make her a desirable acquaintance to Fanny.

"I thank you very warmly for your kind consent to my application, and the kind hint which followed it. I was previously aware of what I should be laying myself open to; but the truth is that the secret has spread so far as to be scarcely the shadow of a secret now, and that, I believe, whenever the third appears, I shall not even attempt to tell lies about it. I shall rather try to make all the money than all the mystery I can of it. People shall pay for their knowledge if I can make them. Henry heard P. and P. warmly praised in Scotland by Lady Robert Kerr and another lady; and what does he do, in the warmth of his brotherly vanity and love, but immediately tell them who wrote it. A thing once set going in that way—one knows how it spreads, and he, dear creature, has set it going so much more than once. I know it is all done from affection and partiality, but at the same time let me here again express to you and Mary my sense of the *superior* kindness which you have shown on the occasion

Another Letter from Jane

in doing what I wished. I am trying to harden myself. After all, what a trifle it is, in all its bearings, to the really important points of one's existence, even in this world.

"I take it for granted that Mary has told you of ——'s engagement to ——. It came upon us without much preparation; at the same time there was that about her which kept us in a constant preparation for something. We are anxious to have it go on well, there being quite as much in his favour as the chances are likely to give her in any matrimonial connection. I believe he is sensible, certainly very religious, well connected, and with some independence. There is an unfortunate dissimilarity of taste between them in one respect, which gives us some apprehensions; he hates company, and she is very fond of it; this, with some queerness of temper on his side, and much unsteadiness on hers, is untoward. I hope Edward's family visit to Chawton will be yearly; he certainly means it now, but we must not expect it to exceed *two* months in future. I do not think, however, that he found five too long this summer. He was very happy there. The new paint improves their house much, and we find no evil from the smell. Poor Mr. Trimmer is lately dead, a sad loss to his family, and occasioning some anxiety to our brother; for the present he continues his affairs in the son's hands, a matter of great importance to *them*. I hope he will have no reason to remove his business.

"Your very affectionate sister,

"J. A.

"There is to be a second edition of S. and S. Egerton advises it."

At the time when this letter was written Charles was on the *Namur*, as Flag-Captain to Sir Thomas Williams. His wife and two small children lived with him on board, an arrangement of somewhat doubtful advantage. In the published letters of Jane Austen there are some of the same date as this one to Frank, written to Cassandra from Godmersham, and giving an account of the visit of Charles and family which she was expecting in October.

"*September* 23.—Wrote to Charles yesterday, and Fanny has had a letter from him to-day, principally to make inquiries about the time of their visit here, to which mine was an answer beforehand; so he will probably write again soon to fix his week."

"*October* 14.—A letter from Wrotham yesterday offering an early visit here, and Mr. and Mrs. Moore and one child are to come on Monday for ten days. I hope Charles and Fanny may not fix the same time, but if they

Another Letter from Jane

come at all in October they must. What is the use of hoping? The two parties of children is the chief evil."

"To be sure, here we are; the very thing has happened, or rather worse—a letter from Charles this very morning, which gives us reason to suppose they may come here to-day. It depends upon the weather, and the weather now is very fine. No difficulties are made, however, and, indeed, there will be no want of room; but I wish there was no Wigrams and Lushingtons in the way to fill up the table, and make us such a motley set. I cannot spare Mr. Lushington either because of his frank, but Mr. Wigram does no good to anybody. I cannot imagine how a man can have the impudence to come into a family party for three days, where he is quite a stranger, unless he knows himself to be agreeable on undoubted authority. I shall be most happy to see dear Charles."

"*Friday, October* 15.—They came last night at about seven. We had given them up, but I still expected them to come. Dessert was nearly over; a better time for arriving than an hour and a half earlier. They were late because they did not set out earlier, and did not allow time enough. Charles did not *aim* at more than reaching Sittingbourne by three, which could not have brought them here by dinner-time. They had a very rough passage ; he would not have ventured if he had known how bad it would be.

" However, here they are, safe and well, just like their own nice selves, Fanny looking as neat and white this morning as possible, and dear Charles all affectionate, placid, quiet, cheerful good humour. They are both looking well, but poor little Cassy is grown extremely thin and looks poorly. I hope a week's country air and exercise may do her good. I am sorry to say it can be but a week. The baby does not appear so large in proportion as she was, nor quite so pretty, but I have seen very little of her. Cassy was too tired and bewildered just at first to seem to know anybody. We met them in the hall, the women and girl part of us, but before we reached the library she kissed me very affectionately, and has since seemed to recollect me in the same way. It was quite an evening of confusion, as you may suppose. At first we were all walking about from one part of the house to the other, then came a fresh dinner in the breakfast-room for Charles and his wife, which Fanny and I attended. Then we moved into the library, were joined by the dining-room people, were introduced, and so forth ; and then we had tea and coffee, which was not over till past ten. Billiards again drew all the odd ones away, and Edward, Charles, the two Fannies, and I sat

MRS. CHARLES AUSTEN

Another Letter from Jane

snugly talking. I shall be glad to have our numbers a little reduced, and by the time you receive this we shall be only a family, though a large family, party.

" I talked to Cassy about Chawton (Cassandra wished to have her there for the winter). She remembers much, but does not volunteer on the subject. Papa and mamma have not yet made up their minds as to parting with her or not; the chief, indeed the only difficulty with mamma is a very reasonable one, the child's being very unwilling to leave them. When it was mentioned to her she did not like the idea of it at all. At the same time she has been suffering so much lately from sea-sickness that her mamma cannot bear to have her much on board this winter. Charles is less inclined to part with her. I do not know how it will end, or what is to determine it. He desires best love to you, and has not written because he has not been able to decide. They are both very sensible of your kindness on the occasion. I have made Charles furnish me with something to say about young Kendall. He is going on very well. When he first joined the *Namur* my brother did not find him forward enough to be what they call put in the office, and therefore placed him under the schoolmaster, and he is very much improved, and goes into the office now every afternoon, still attending school in the morning."

This is interesting as an example of the way in which the young men learnt their work as midshipmen.

The domestic side of Charles' character is always rather inclined to obtrude itself. Perhaps it was of him that Jane was thinking when Admiral Croft sums up James Benwick in the words, " ' An excellent, good-hearted fellow I assure you, a very active, zealous officer, too, which is more than you would think for perhaps, for that soft sort of manner does not do him justice ; " and when later on she protests against the " too common idea of spirit and gentleness being incompatible with each other." Nevertheless, we have ample proof that both sisters thought his domesticity somewhat overdone, though it is hardly fair to quote even friendly criticism of such an intimate nature. One sentence from a letter on October 18 gives the hint of what seems to have been Charles' one defect in the eyes of his sisters.

" I think I have just done a good deed—extracted Charles from his wife and children upstairs, and made him get ready to go out shooting, and not keep Mr. Moore waiting any longer."

Before Jane's death in 1817, Charles had opportunity to show the stuff of which he was made, and from that time till his death in 1852, under

254

Another Letter from Jane

circumstances which called for great courage and endurance, he fully realised her best hopes.

The question of Cassy living with her father and mother on the *Namur* reminds one of the discussion in " Persuasion " as to the comforts of ladies on board ship.

" The admiral, after taking two or three refreshing turns about the room with his hands behind him, being called to order by his wife, now came up to Captain Wentworth, and without any observation of what he might be interrupting, thinking only of his own thoughts, began with—' If you had been a week later at Lisbon, last spring, Frederick, you would have been asked to give a passage to Lady Mary Grierson and her daughters.'

" ' Should I ?   I am glad I was not a week later then.' "

The admiral abused him for his want of gallantry.   He defended himself, though professing that he would never willingly admit any ladies on board a ship of his, excepting for a ball, or a visit, which a few hours might comprehend.   " But, if I know myself," said he, " this is from no want of gallantry towards them.   It is rather from feeling how impossible it is, with all one's efforts and all one's sacrifices, to make the accommodations on board such as women ought to have.   There can be no want of gallantry, admiral, in rating the claims of women to every personal comfort high, and this is what I do. I hate to hear of women on board, or to see them on board, and no ship under my command shall ever convey a family of ladies anywhere if I can help it.'"

This brought his sister upon him.

"'Oh, Frederick! But I cannot believe it of you. All idle refinement! Women may be as comfortable on board as in the best house in England. I believe I have lived as much on board as most women, and I know nothing superior to the accommodation of a man-of-war. I declare I have not a comfort or an indulgence about me, even at Kellynch Hall' (with a kind bow to Anne), 'beyond what I always had in most of the ships I have lived in, and they have been five altogether.'

"'Nothing to the purpose,' replied her brother. "You were living with your husband, and were the only woman on board.'

"'But you, yourself, brought Mrs. Harville, her sister, her cousin, and the three children round from Portsmouth to Plymouth. Where was this superfine, extraordinary sort of gallantry of yours then?'

"'All merged in my friendship, Sophia. I would assist any brother officer's wife that I could, and I would bring anything of Harville's from the world's end, if he wanted it. But do not imagine that I did not feel it an evil, in itself.'

Another Letter from Jane

" ' Depend upon it, they were all perfectly comfortable.'

" ' I might not like them the better for that, perhaps. Such a number of women and children have no right to be comfortable on board.'

" ' My dear Frederick, you are talking quite idly. Pray, what would become of us poor sailors' wives, who often want to be conveyed to one port or another, after our husbands, if everybody had your feelings.'

" ' My feelings you see did not prevent my taking Mrs. Harville and all her family to Plymouth.'

" ' But I hate to hear you talking so like a fine gentleman, and as if women were all fine ladies, instead of rational creatures. We none of us expect to be in smooth water all our days.'

" ' Ah, my dear,' said the Admiral, ' when he has got a wife he will sing a different tune. When he is married, if we have the good luck to live to another war, we shall see him do as you and I, and a great many others, have done. We shall have him very thankful to anybody that will bring him his wife.'

" ' Ay, that we shall.'

" ' Now I have done,' cried Captain Wentworth. When once married people begin to attack me with—" Oh, you will think very differently when you are married," I can only say, " No, I shall not," and then they say again, " Yes, you will," and there is an end of it.'

" He got up and moved away.

" ' What a great traveller you must have been, ma'am,' said Mrs. Musgrove to Mrs. Croft.

" ' Pretty well, ma'am, in the fifteen years of my marriage, though many women have done more. I have crossed the Atlantic four times, and have been once to the East Indies and back again, and only once ;. besides being in different places about home : Cork, and Lisbon, and Gibraltar. But I never went beyond the Straits, and was never in the West Indies. We do not call Bermuda or Bahama, you know, the West Indies.'

" Mrs. Musgrove had not a word to say in dissent : she could not accuse herself of having ever called them anything in the whole course of her life.

" ' And I do assure you, ma'am,' pursued Mrs. Croft, 'that nothing can exceed the accommodations of a man-of-war. I speak, you know, of the higher rates. When you come to a frigate, of course you are more confined; though any reasonable woman may be perfectly happy in one of them ; and I can safely say that the happiest part of my life has been spent on board a ship. While we were together, you know, there was nothing to be feared. Thank God ! I have always been blessed with excellent health, and no climate dis-

Another Letter from Jane

agrees with me. The only time that I ever really suffered in body and mind, the only time that I ever fancied myself unwell, or had any ideas of danger, was the winter that I passed by myself at Deal, when the Admiral (Captain Croft then) was in the North Seas. I lived in perpetual fright at that time, and had all manner of imaginary complaints from not knowing what to do with myself, or when I should hear from him next ; but as long as we could be together, nothing ever ailed me, and I never met with the smallest inconvenience.'

" ' Ay, to be sure. Yes, indeed, oh yes. I am quite of your opinion, Mrs. Croft,' was Mrs. Musgrove's hearty answer. ' There is nothing so bad as a separation. I am quite of your opinion. I know what it is, for Mr. Musgrove always attends the assizes, and I am so glad when they are over, and he is safe back again.' "

CHAPTER XVII

THE END OF THE WAR

In the letter quoted in the last chapter, we hear how Henry let out the secret of Jane's authorship. She has also something to say to Cassandra about the matter. "Lady Robert Kerr is delighted with P. and P., and really was so, as I understand, before she knew who wrote it, for, of course she knows now. He (Henry) told her with as much satisfaction as if it were my wish. He did not tell me this, but he told Fanny." Perhaps the pleasure that she gained in hearing how people enjoyed her books partly made up for the annoyance of having her wishes for secrecy forgotten. She goes on : "And Mr. Hastings, I am quite delighted with what such a man writes about it. Henry sent him the books after his return from Daylesford, but *you* will hear the letter too." This is tantalising for those who cannot hear the letter too, and still more so when she adds later on : "I long to have you hear Mr. H.'s opinion of P. and P. His admiring my

The End of the War

Elizabeth so much is particularly welcome to me."

The interest of Warren Hastings in the Austen family was a long-standing one. Hastings' only son was brought up under the care of Jane's father and mother at Steventon. When he died, in early manhood, the grief of Mrs. Austen was as great as if she had lost one of her own children. Probably they were entrusted with the care of this boy through the influence of George Austen's sister, who was married to Dr. Hancock, of Calcutta, a close friend of Warren Hastings. Their daughter, Eliza Hancock, after losing her first husband, a French count, under the guillotine in the Reign of Terror, married Henry Austen. She died in 1813, and Henry's loss was a subject of much concern in the family. We can see this from Jane's letters at the time to Cassandra, and in the one to Frank quoted at length in the last chapter, where she expresses her belief that Henry's mind is not " a mind for affliction."

Frank got home from the Baltic early in 1814. We hear of him in June trying to arrange for a visit to his mother. Jane writes: " I heard yesterday from Frank. When he began his letter he hoped to be here on Monday, but before it was ended he had been told that the naval review would not take place till Friday, which would probably occasion him some delay, as he cannot

Jane Austen's Sailor Brothers

get some necessary business of his own attended to while Portsmouth is in such a bustle." Her books seem to have become more and more of a family interest. Mentions of them come in constantly in the midst of all the family gossip. "Sweet amiable Frank, why does he have a cold too? Like Captain Mirvan to Mr. Duval. 'I wish it well over with him.' Thank you very much for the sight of dearest Charles's letter to yourself. How pleasant and naturally he writes, and how perfect a picture of his disposition and feeling his style conveys! Poor fellow! Not a present! I have a great mind to send him all the twelve copies (of "Emma"), which were to have been dispersed among my near connections, beginning with the Prince Regent and ending with Countess Morley." The mention of Miss Burney's "Evelina" is characteristic. It was one of her favourite books.

On Frank's return he naturally wishes to settle somewhere with his wife and family after so many years afloat, but he did not at once find the sort of home he wanted. He occupied Chawton Great House for a few years, but this was only a temporary arrangement. It must be one of the chief pleasures of a novelist to bestow upon her characters all the blessings which she would like to portion out to her friends. Perhaps it was something of this feeling which induced Jane to

The End of the War

draw the ideal home of a naval man in "Persuasion." Certainly in tastes and feelings there is much similarity between Harville and Frank Austen.

"Captain Harville had taken his present house for half a year ; his taste, and his health, and his fortune, all directing him to a residence unexpensive, and by the sea ; and the grandeur of the country, and the retirement of Lyme in the winter, appeared exactly adapted to ¦Captain Benwick's state of mind. Nothing could be more pleasant than their desire of considering the whole party as friends of their own, because the friends of Captain Wentworth, or more kindly hospitable than their entreaties for their all promising to dine with them. The dinner, already ordered at the inn, was at last, though unwillingly, accepted as an excuse, but they seemed almost hurt that Captain Wentworth should have brought such a party to Lyme, without considering it as a thing of course that they should dine with them.

"There was so much attachment to Captain Wentworth in all this, and such a bewitching charm in a degree of hospitality so uncommon, so unlike the usual style of give-and-take invitations, and dinners of formality and display, that Anne felt her spirits not likely to be benefited by an increasing acquaintance among his brother officers. ' These would all have been my friends,' was her

thought, and she had to struggle against a great
tendency to lowness.

"On quitting the Cobb they all went indoors
with their new friends, and found rooms so small
as none but those who invite from the heart could
think capable of accommodating so many. Anne
had a moment's astonishment on the subject
herself, but it was soon lost in the pleasant feelings
which sprang from the sight of all the ingenious
contrivances and nice arrangements of Captain
Harville to turn the actual space to the best possible account, to supply the deficiencies of lodging-
house furniture, and defend the windows and doors
against the winter storms to be expected. The
varieties in the fitting up of the rooms, where the
common necessaries provided by the owner, in
the common indifferent plight, were contrasted
with some few articles of a rare species of wood,
excellently worked up, and with something
curious and valuable from all the distant countries
Captain Harville had visited, were more than
amusing to Anne; connected as it all was with
his profession, the fruit of its labours, the effect
of its influence on his habits, the picture of repose
and domestic happiness it presented, made it to
her a something more or less than gratification.

"Captain Harville was no reader; but he had
contrived excellent accommodations, and fashioned
very pretty shelves, for a tolerable collection of

The End of the War

well-bound volumes, the property of Captain Benwick. His lameness prevented him from taking much exercise; but a mind of usefulness and ingenuity seemed to furnish him with constant employment within. He drew, he varnished, he carpentered, he glued; he made toys for the children; he fashioned new netting-needles and pins with improvements; and if everything else was done, sat down to his large fishing-net at one corner of the room.

" Anne thought she left great happiness behind her when they quitted the house; and Louisa, by whom she found herself walking, burst forth into raptures of admiration and delight on the character of the Navy, their friendliness, their brotherliness, their openness, their uprightness; protesting that she was convinced of sailors having more worth and warmth than any other set of men in England; that they only knew how to live, and they only deserved to be respected and loved."

No one reading " Persuasion " could doubt that, ready as Jane always was to laugh at absurdities of fashion, yet the national enthusiasm for the Navy had not failed to touch her heart any more that it had missed her sense of humour. Trying as Louisa's encomium must have been to Anne, with her mind full of regrets over her broken engagement with Captain Wentworth, it

Jane Austen's Sailor Brothers

was the inward agreement of her mind with this admiration for simplicity and affection which gave her the worst pain. The nation had passed through a crisis, and after the stress of war, the happy family life was the one thing admirable.

Captain Charles Austen had spent ten years on active service, outside the theatre of hostilities, but now he was brought into closer touch during the confusion caused by the escape of Napoleon from Elba. The *Phœnix* frigate under his command was sent with the *Undaunted* and the *Garland* in pursuit of a Neapolitan squadron cruising in the Adriatic. Since 1808 Naples had been under the rule of Murat, Napoleon's brother-in-law. It was, therefore, Murat's flag which was attacked by the British men-of-war.

Joachim Murat's history is a curiously romantic one. As his dealings with Napoleon created the situation in Naples which called for British interference, it will not be a digression to give some account of him. His origin was a low one, and it was chiefly as the husband of Napoleon's sister Caroline that he came to the front. As a soldier his talents were great, but he was no diplomatist, and too impetuous and unstable to be successful. He fought under Napoleon in most of the campaigns from Marengo to Leipzig, and first entered Naples as the victorious general of the French army. In 1808, at a time when Napoleon was

CAPTAIN CHARLES AUSTEN, C.B.

The End of the War

giving away kingdoms, Joseph Bonaparte, the
King of Naples, was awarded the somewhat empty
and unsatisfactory honour of the kingdom of
Spain ; and at the same time, to take his place,
Murat was raised to the dignity of " King of the
Two Sicilies." The Bourbon King Ferdinand,
who bore the same title, had been maintained in
power in the island of Sicily by the British fleet
ever since Nelson's time. Murat's great idea was
the unity of Italy, under himself as King, and he
perhaps had hopes that Napoleon would support
him. At all events, he was loyal to the Emperor
until 1811, when he went to Paris for the baptism
of Napoleon's son, but came away before the
ceremony on learning that the infant was to be
" King of Rome." He dismissed his French
troops, and resolved to govern without reference
to Napoleon. Unable, however, to resist a call to
arms from his former chief, in 1812 he went to
Russia in command of the heavy cavalry, and was
the first to cross the frontier. He went twenty
leagues beyond Moscow, and finally left the army
on the retreat at the Oder. He handed over the
command to Eugène Beauharnais, and returned to
Naples.

Among others who saw that Napoleon's power
was on the wane, Murat now turned against him,
and proposed, through Lord William Bentinck at
Palermo, a treaty of peace with England, on

the basis of the unification of Italy under his own sovereignty. This agreement was made, and needed only the formal consent of the British Government, when Murat suddenly threw it all over, and at Napoleon's bidding went off to fight for him in the campaign of 1813 at Dresden and Leipzig. On his return, however, the King again began his negotiations with the allies, and arranged a treaty with Austria. The Congress of Vienna debated the question of allowing him to remain King. As matters stood, it was difficult to find a reason for turning him out, as he now appeared to have definitely abandoned the Emperor's cause. But, naturally, it was impossible to repose much confidence in his assertions. He himself seems scarcely to have known his own mind, and was ready to ally himself with either side, if by that means he could secure his heart's desire of the kingdom of Italy. His wife cared more for her brother's cause than for her husband's, but Joachim trusted her completely. They had for long kept up the appearance of disagreement, in order to collect round them the leaders of all parties ; and now when the dissension was real, he hardly realised how little her sympathies were with him. It seems not unlikely that England and Austria would have trusted him, and allowed him to retain his throne, as, on the whole, he had governed well ; but he himself decided the ques-

The End of the War

tion in a characteristic way. He had tidings of
Napoleon's projected escape from Elba, and
espoused his cause. The kingdom of the Two
Sicilies was thereupon attacked by the allies,
and before Waterloo was fought the Bourbon
King Ferdinand was reinstated at Naples under
the protection of the fleets. Queen Caroline,
Murat's wife, was escorted by British sailors from
the palace. The ship bearing her away passed
another British ship, which brought Ferdinand
back to his capital.

The city of Naples had surrendered, but
Brindisi still held out. It was here that Charles
Austen was employed in blockading the port as
Captain of the *Phœnix*, with the *Garland* under
his orders. After a short time negotiations were
begun, and, without much serious fighting, he
induced the garrison of the castle and the commanders of the two frigates in the port to hoist the
white flag of the Bourbons, in place of the crim-
son and white on a blue ground which Joachim
Murat had adopted. It is a matter of history
how Murat, with a few followers, attempted to set
up this flag again a few months later in Calabria,
but was taken prisoner and shot. It is evident
that his estrangement from Napoleon originated
with the title of " King of Rome " being conferred
on the boy born in 1811—a clear indication that
the Emperor was no party to his schemes of

uniting Italy. Whether or not the change of monarchs was a good one for the Neapolitan people, the restored kingdom of the Two Sicilies lasted until Garibaldi caused its complete collapse in 1860, and accomplished Murat's ideal for Italy.

After this episode Captain Charles Austen was kept busy with Greek pirates in the Archipelago until the *Phœnix* was lost off Smyrna in 1816. He then returned to England.

There is an extract from one of his letters to Jane at this time, dated May 6, 1815, from Palermo, which shows something of the degree of popularity which her books had then attained. "Books became the subject of conversation, and I praised 'Waverley' highly, when a young man present observed that nothing had come out for years to be compared with 'Pride and Prejudice,' 'Sense and Sensibility,' &c. As I am sure you must be anxious to know the name of a person of so much taste, I shall tell you it is Fox, a nephew of the late Charles James Fox. That you may not be too much elated at this morsel of praise, I shall add that he did not appear to like 'Mansfield Park' so well as the two first, in which, however, I believe he is singular."

Early in 1816 Jane's health began to fail, and she grew gradually weaker until she died, in July 1817. There is a letter from her to Charles, dated from Chawton on April 6, 1817, which is

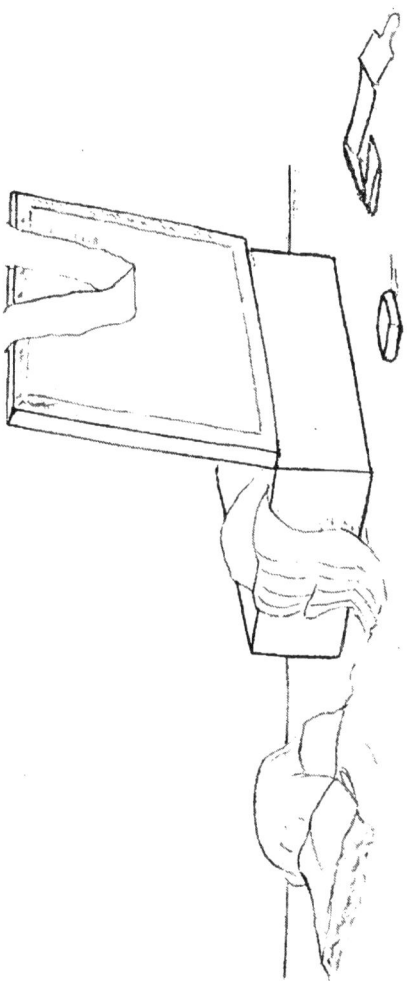

JANE AUSTEN'S WORK-BOX, WITH HER LAST PIECE OF WORK

The End of the War

inscribed in his handwriting, " My last letter
from dearest Jane." It is full of courage, even
through its weariness. Most of it relates to
purely family matters, but the tenor of it all is
the same—that of patient cheerfulness :

" My dearest Charles,—Many thanks for
your affectionate letter. I was in your debt
before, but I have really been too unwell the last
fortnight to write anything that was not absolutely necessary. . . . There was no standing
Mrs. Cooke's affectionate way of speaking of
your countenance, after her seeing you. God
bless you all. Conclude me to be going on well,
if you hear nothing to the contrary.
" Yours ever truly,
" J. A.
" Tell dear Harriet that whenever she wants
me in her service again she must send a Hackney
Chariot all the way for me, for I am not strong
enough to travel any other way, and I hope
Cassy will take care that it is a green one."

Both Francis and Charles Austen were at
home at the time of Jane's death in 1817.
In the May before she died she was prevailed
upon to go to Winchester, to be under the
care of Mr. Lyford, a favourite doctor in that
part. She and Cassandra lived in College Street.

Jane Austen's Sailor Brothers

She had always been fond of Winchester—in the true "Jane Austen spirit," partly because her nephews were at school there—and her keen interest in her surroundings did not desert her even now, when she, and all around her, knew that she was dying. A set of verses, written only three days before her death, though of no great merit in themselves, have a value quite their own in showing that her unselfish courage and cheerfulness never failed her. Only a few hours after writing them she had a turn for the worse, and died early on the morning of July 18.

"WINCHESTER, *July* 15, 1817.

" When Winchester races first took their beginning
　　'Tis said that the people forgot their old saint,
　That they never applied for the leave of St. Swithun,
　　And that William of Wykeham's approval was faint.

" The races however were fixed and determined,
　　The company met, and the weather was charming;
　The lords and the ladies were satined and ermined,
　　And nobody saw any future alarming.

" But when the old saint was informed of their doings,
　　He made but one spring from his shrine to the roof
　Of the palace that now stands so sadly in ruins,
　　And thus he addressed them, all standing aloof:

"' Oh, subject rebellious ! Oh, Venta depraved !
　　When once we are buried you think we are dead ;
　But behold me immortal—by vice you're enslaved,
　　You have sinned, and must suffer,' then further he said—

272

The End of the War

"'These races, and revels, and dissolute measures,
  With which you're debasing a neighbouring plain;
 Let them stand—you shall meet with a curse in your pleasures.
  Set off for your course. I'll pursue with my rain.

"'You cannot but know my command o'er July;
  Thenceforward I'll triumph in showing my powers;
 Shift your race as you will, it shall never be dry,
  The curse upon Venta is July in showers.'"

CHAPTER XVIII

TWO ADMIRALS

WE have shown, so far as is possible, the influence that the lives of her two sailor brothers had upon the writings of Jane Austen. It now only remains to show how both of them, in their different ways, fulfilled her hopes for them. This can be best done by a brief summary of the chief events in their careers. At the time of her death they were men on either side of forty. Francis lived to be ninety-one, and Charles to be seventy-three, so both had many more years of activity and service before them.

In 1826 Charles was again on the West Indies station. Here he stayed for more than two years, and was chiefly employed in suppressing the slave-trade. He was always very happy in the management of crews. It was partly owing to his more than usual care in this respect while stationed here on board the *Aurora*, and partly to his general activity as second in command, that he gained his appointment as Flag-Captain to

Mem? 12th May 1838

The Officers of the watch on board H.M.S. Bellerophon are directed to pay strict attention to the orders which will be inserted in this book for their governance during the Night

Charles Mc Austin Captain

Two Admirals

Admiral Colpoys in the *Winchester* on the same station in 1828. He was invalided home in 1830, as the result of a severe accident. This prevented him from being again employed until 1838, when he was appointed to the *Bellerophon*, still only a Captain after nearly thirty years' service in that rank.

Some years before this, Mehemet Ali, Pasha of Egypt, had conquered Syria from his Suzerain, the Sultan, and now wished to declare himself independent, thereby coming into collision with the traditional policy of England and France in the Levant. In 1840 Admiral Stopford's fleet was sent to the coast of Syria to interfere with communications between the Pasha's army and Egypt. Charles Austen in the *Bellerophon* (called by the seamen the "Billy Ruffian") took part in the bombardment of the Beyrout forts, and afterwards was stationed in one of the neighbouring bays, guarding the entrance of the pass by which Commodore Sir Charles Napier had advanced up the Lebanon to attack Ibrahim Pasha and the Egyptians. In Napier's words : "It was rather a new occurrence for a British Commodore to be on the top of Mount Lebanon commanding a Turkish army, and preparing to fight a battle which should decide the fate of Syria." He won the battle and returned to the *Powerful*, with some reluctance, making way for Colonel Smith, who was appointed by the Sultan to command his forces in Syria.

The Admiral and Colonel Smith shortly afterwards decided on capturing Acre, the chief stronghold now remaining in the Egyptian occupation.

In a letter to Lord Palmerston, Colonel Smith describes the action : " On October 26 it was finally determined between Sir Robert Stopford and myself that the siege of Acre should be undertaken. Owing to the light winds the ships did not get into action till 2 P.M. on November 3, when an animated fire commenced, and was maintained without intermission until darkness closed the operations of the day. About three hours later the Governor, with a portion of the garrison, quitted the town, which was taken possession of by the allied troops at daylight the following morning. The moral influence on the cause in which we are engaged that will result from its surrender is incalculable. During the bombardment the principal magazine and the whole arsenal blew up."

There is an extract from Charles Austen's journal, which also gives a slight account of the bombardment :

" 9 A.M.—Received a note from the Admiral (Stopford) telling me the *Powerful* (Commodore Napier) was to lead into action, followed by *Princess Charlotte* (flag), *Bellerophon* and *Thun-*

derer, who were all to lay against the Western Wall.

"*Later.*—Working up to the attack with light airs.

"11.30.—Piped to dinner.

"1 P.M.—Bore up to our station, passing outside the shoal to the south, and then to the westward again inside.

"2.30.—Anchored astern of the *Princess Charlotte*, and abreast of the Western Castle, and immediately commenced firing, which the enemy returned, but they fired high, and only two shots hulled us, hitting no one.

"*At sunset.*.—Admiral signalled 'Cease firing,' up boats, and then piped to supper, and sat down with the two boys to a cold fowl, which we enjoyed much.

"*At* 9 P.M.—A dish of tea, then gave my night orders and turned in."

The "two boys" were his two sons, Charles and Henry, who were serving under him.

There is a further account of a difficulty with Commodore Napier, who had a firm belief in his own judgment, which made obedience to orders something of a trial to him. Napier, who was "as usual a law unto himself," disobeyed the Admiral's signals, and, when reprimanded, demanded a court-martial, which was refused. The journal then relates that Captain Austen, with two

other captains, went on board the *Powerful* to
endeavour to persuade the Commodore to climb
down, "but the old Commodore was stubborn,
and we returned to our ships." However, a second
visit to the Commodore in the afternoon appears
to have been more successful, and " I left hoping
the affair would be settled," which it was. The
result of this bombardment was altogether satisfactory, though some of the ships suffered considerably from the Egyptian firing. Charles was
awarded a Companionship of the Bath for his
share in this campaign.

In 1846 he became Rear-Admiral, and in 1850
was appointed Commander-in-Chief on the East
India Station.

He left England in the P. & O. steamer *Ripon*
for Alexandria, and crossed the desert to Suez,
as was usual in the overland route. The description of the mode of travelling by vans, and the
selection of places therein by lot, has often been
made.

Lord Dalhousie, as Governor-General at Calcutta, had taken steps to protect British traders
from the exactions of the Burmese officials at
Rangoon by sending a Commission of Inquiry,
with power to demand reparation. The Commissioner (Commodore Lambert) decided to treat
only with the King of Ava, who consented, in
January 1852, to remove the Governor from

REAR-ADMIRAL CHARLES AUSTEN, C.B.

Two Admirals

Rangoon. This action did not, however, prove effectual in settling the grievances, and Commodore Lambert declared the Burmese coast in a state of blockade; his vessel was fired upon, and he retaliated by destroying a stockade on the river-bank, and some Burmese war-boats. Shortly afterwards he received orders to forward to the King a despatch of Lord Dalhousie's, demanding apology and an indemnity. The same vessel again went up the river with the despatch, and was attacked by the Burmese. The Governor-General thereupon ordered a combined military and naval expedition, which was on the coast by the end of March. This was to be the last of Charles Austen's many enterprises. He shifted his flag from the *Hastings* to the steam sloop *Rattler* at Trincomalee in Ceylon, and proceeded to the mouth of the Rangoon river. On April 3, accompanied by two ships and the necessary troops, he was on his way to Martaban, which they attacked and captured on the 5th. The place was held by 5000 men; but after a bombardment of an hour and a half it was taken by storm with small loss.

On the 10th began a general combined movement on Rangoon, which fell on the 14th, the *Rattler* taking a leading part in attacking the outlying stockades. The large stockade round the town and the pagoda was carried at the point of the bayonet. The navy suffered but little loss from the enemy; but cholera set in, and the Admiral fell ill. He was persuaded by the doctors to leave the river, as all active proceedings of the expedition had ceased for the time. He went to Calcutta, where, through the kind hospitality of the Governor-General, he gradually recovered his health. Rangoon, with its wonderful solid pagoda, and all its Buddhist traditions, was now in British hands; but the Burmese Government were bent on recapturing it, for certain royal offerings to the shrine were among the conditions of the King's tenure of his throne. The war was therefore continued, and it was decided to penetrate further up the river, and with a yet stronger force. Admiral Austen thereupon returned to duty. On arrival at Rangoon in the *Hastings* he transferred his flag to the steam sloop *Pluto*, and went up the river on a reconnaissance, in advance of the combined forces. The main body proceeded direct to Henzada, by the principal channel of the Irrawadi, while the contingent following the *Pluto* was delayed by the resistance of the Burmese leader at Donabyu. It became necessary for the main body to make for this point also, while Admiral Austen was by this time much further north, at Prome. He was anxiously awaiting their arrival, while his health grew worse during the two or three weeks spent in this

unhealthy region. On October 6, his last notes at
Prome are as follows: "Received a report that
two steamers had been seen at anchor some miles
below, wrote this and a letter to my wife, and
read the lessons of the day." On the following
morning he died. The Burmese leader was also
killed during the assault, which took place at
Donabyu not long afterwards, and his army then
retreated. The British battalions were eventually
quartered on the hill above Prome, overlooking
the wide river, not far from Lord Dalhousie's new
frontier of Lower Burmah. Now thick jungle
covers alike the camp and the site of the fort of
Donabyu (White Peacock Town), for Upper
Burmah is British too, and there is no king to
make offerings at the Rangoon shrine.

The death of Charles was a heavy blow to
Francis. The only other survivor of all his brothers and sisters, Edward Knight, of Godmersham
and Chawton, died at about the same time;
but Francis had still thirteen years of life
before him. To realise what his life had been
we must return to the close of the long war, when
he came on shore from the *Elephant*, and was not
called upon to go to sea again for thirty years.
It is easy to imagine the changes that had taken
place in the Navy in the interval between his times
of active service.

During these years on shore several honours

fell to his share. He had been awarded his C.B. in 1815, on the institution of that distinction. In 1825 he was appointed Colonel of Marines, and in 1830 Rear-Admiral. About the same time he purchased Portsdown Lodge, where he lived for the rest of his life. This property is now included within the lines of forts for the defence of Portsmouth, and was bought for that purpose by the Government some years before his death. At the last investiture by King William IV. in 1837 he received the honour of K.C.B. ; and the next year, on the occasion of Queen Victoria's Coronation, he was promoted to the rank of Vice-Admiral. In 1845 he took command of the North American and West Indies Station. This command in the *Vindictive* forms a notable contrast to his earlier experiences in the West Indies. How often he must have called to mind as he visited Barbadoes, Jamaica, or Antigua, the excitements of the *Canopus* cruises of forty years ago ! How different too the surroundings had become with the regular English mail service, and the paddle-wheel sloops of war in place of brigs such as the *Curieux* —and, greatest change of all, no such urgent services to be performed as that of warning England against the approach of an enemy's fleet !

Nevertheless, there was plenty to be done. The Naval Commander-in-Chief has no easy berth,

Two Admirals

even in time of peace. His letters tell us of some of the toils which fell to his share.

"Our passage from Bermuda was somewhat tedious; we left it on February 6, called oft Antigua on the 15th, and, without anchoring the ship, I landed for an hour to inspect the naval yard," rather an exertion in the tropics, for a man of seventy-three. A voyage to La Guayra follows. It appears that Venezuela was giving as much trouble in 1848 as in 1900.

"A political question is going on between the Government of Caraccas and our Chargé d'affaires, and a British force is wanted to give weight to our arguments. I am afraid it will detain us a good while, as I also hear that there is a demand for a ship-of-war to protect property from apprehended outrage in consequence of a revolutionary insurrection."

We find that the *Vindictive* was at Jamaica within a fortnight or so. It would appear that the Government of the Caraccas (legitimate or revolutionary) was quickly convinced by the weight of the arguments of a 50-gun ship.

The following general memorandum may be interesting with reference to the expedition against Greytown, Nicaragua.

"The Vice-Admiral Commander-in-Chief has much gratification in signifying to the squadron the high sense he entertains of the gallantry and good conduct of Captain Loch, of her Majesty's ship *Alarm*, and of every officer and man of her Majesty's ships *Alarm* and *Vixen*, and of the officers and soldiers of her Majesty's 28th Regiment, employed under his orders on the expedition up the river St. Juan, and especially for the cool and steady intrepidity evinced while under a galling fire from a nearly invisible enemy on the morning of February 12, and the irresistible bravery with which the works of Serapagui were stormed and carried. The result has been an additional proof that valour, when well directed and regulated by discipline, will never fail in effecting its object."

There are also notes about the Mexican and United States War then in progress, and instructions to treat Mexican privateers severely if they interfered with neutral craft. Strong measures were also to be enforced against slave-traders, who still sailed under Brazilian and Portuguese flags, but were now reprobated by international treaties generally.

In May 1848 the *Vindictive* was met by Vice-Admiral the Earl of Dundonald in the *Wellesley*. Lord Dundonald was to take over the command from Sir Francis. We have no record of any meeting between these two officers since the days when Lord Cochrane in the *Speedy* and Captain Austen in the *Peterel* were in the Mediterranean

SIR FRANCIS AUSTEN, G.C.B., ADMIRAL OF THE FLEET

Two Admirals

together, almost half a century earlier. Sir
Francis' letters mention with pleasure the desire
on the part of his successor to continue matters
on the same lines.

His return to England was coincident with
promotion to the rank of Admiral. In 1854, at
the outbreak of the Crimean War, the Portsmouth
command was declined as too onerous for an
octogenarian.

In 1860 Sir Francis received the G.C.B., and
in 1862 the successive honours of Rear-Admiral
and Vice-Admiral of the United Kingdom, followed in 1863 by promotion to the senior position
in the British Navy as Admiral of the Fleet.

"THE ADMIRALTY, *April* 27, 1863.

"SIR,—I am happy to acquaint you that I have
had the pleasure of bringing your name before
the Queen for promotion to Admiral of the Fleet,
and that her Majesty has been graciously pleased
to approve of the appointment 'as a well-
deserved reward for your brilliant services.'

"I am, Sir, your most obedient servant,
"SOMERSET."

From the year 1858 Sir Francis had become
gradually less able to move about. He retained
all his faculties and his ability to write, almost as

clearly as ever, until just before his death in August 1865.

The strong sense of justice, manifest in his rigid adherence to discipline as a young man, was tempered later in life by his love for children and grandchildren, constant through so many years.

Of both Jane Austen's brothers it may be said that they were worthy members of that profession which is, "if possible, more distinguished for its domestic virtues than for its national importance."

INDEX

INDEX

289   T

Index

Index

Index

Index

Index

Lightning Source UK Ltd.
Milton Keynes UK
UKHW02f1409260418
321688UK00014B/559/P

9 781116 974300